MEN ARE FROM MARS

Women Are from Venus

BOOK OF DAYS

D0433141

MEN ARE FROM MARS

Women Are from Venus

BOOK OF DAYS

365 Inspirations to Enrich
Your Relationships

JOHN GRAY, Ph.D.

VERMILION
London

1 3 5 7 9 10 8 6 4 2

Copyright © 1998 by Mars Productions, Inc

First published in the US by HarperCollins 1998
This edition published in the United Kingdom in 1999 by Vermilion,
an imprint of Ebury Press
Random House
20 Vauxhall Bridge Road
London SW1V 2SA

Random House Australia (Pty) Limited
20 Alfred Street, Milsons Point, Sydney,
New South Wales 2061, Australia

Random House New Zealand Limited
18 Poland Road, Glenfield,
Auckland 10, New Zealand

Random House South Africa (Pty) Limited
Endulini, 5A Jubilee Road, Parktown 2193, South Africa

Random House UK Limited Reg. No. 954009

A CIP catalogue for this book is available from the British Library

ISBN: 0 09 182710 8

Printed and bound in Great Britain by Mackays of Chatham plc, Kent

DEDICATION

This book is dedicated with deepest love and affection to my wife Bonnie. Her consistent love, support, strength, and wisdom have inspired me day by day to be the best I can be and share what we have learned together.

ACKNOWLEDGMENTS

I thank my wife Bonnie and our three daughters, Shannon, Juliet, and Lauren, for their continuous love and support.

I thank Josie and Martin Brown for their encouragement and excellent editorial assistance in putting this book together.

I thank Diane Reverand at HarperCollins for her brilliant feedback and advice. I also thank Laura Leonard, my dream publicist, Carl Raymond, and the other incredible staff at HarperCollins.

I thank my assistant, Helen Drake, and my staff: Michael Najarian, Donna Doiron, Bart and Merril Berens, Ian and Ellie Coren, Pollyanna Jacobs, Reggie Henkart, and Sandra Weinstein for their consistent support and hard work.

I wish to thank the hundreds of workshop facilitators who teach Mars-Venus Workshops throughout the world, and I thank the thousands of individuals and couples who have participated in these workshops over the past 15 years. I also thank the Mars-Venus Counselors who continue to use these principles in their counseling practices.

A very special thanks to my dear friend Kaleshwar.

INTRODUCTION

*P*ossibly the biggest problem in relationships today is our tendency to assume that our partners are like us. We mistakenly believe that if our partners love us, they will think, feel, and behave in certain ways. If they are bothered by something, we assume that our way of dealing with problems is best for them. This is rarely the case. With a greater understanding of how men and women are different, we can avoid unnecessary frustration and disappointment.

Remembering that men are from Mars and women are from Venus helps us give up our resistance to differences and find acceptance. Rather than succumbing to our tendency to want to change, improve, or fix our partners, we can instead take time to understand them. By remembering that we are *supposed* to be different, we not only find peace and comfort, but we gain the necessary insight to give and receive love successfully with our partners.

The *Men Are from Mars, Women Are from Venus Book of Days* contains 365 daily inspirations to remind you each day of the basic differences between men and women. Reading a short daily reminder is just enough to point you in the right direction toward understanding and working with the differences instead of feeling powerless or stuck.

With this additional support,
every day can be an opportunity to grow in love.

Although the Mars/Venus principles make sense, they are still not easy to remember and put into practice. They are still new. At the times when we need these insights most, we tend to forget. Usually we just need a little reminder to trigger our positive feelings of trust, acceptance, understanding, and appreciation for the opposite sex. By remembering how we are different, we can always come up with a more effective way to give and to get love. As you read one of the short inspirations each day, you will feel supported in your journey of making love and romance a priority in your life.

In the process of learning something new, there is a natural learning curve. With practice and application, new knowledge becomes automatically a part of you.

To master the principles
of the Mars/Venus approach to relationships,
we need to relearn them many times.

My own experience was first discovering these ideas and then putting them into practice. As time passed and problems arose, I realized I had forgotten to put into practice what I had already learned. After refreshing my memory, I changed my behavior, and things were better for a while. Then, once again, problems would come up and I would have to remind myself of the relationship techniques I had forgotten. After several years of this process, most of the ideas I teach have become second nature.

Generally speaking, to learn something completely new takes learning it, forgetting it, and then recognizing that we have forgotten it a number of times. Then it becomes second nature. Well, in this *Book of Days* you will hear it 365 times. By checking in every day for a year, you will give yourself the perfect opportunity to master these new relationship skills.

The *Book of Days* will help remind you of the most important ideas in the Mars/Venus collection. Many of the inspirations are taken directly from my previous books with a few modifications and updates. This book is immediately helpful and supportive to those who have read my other books, but it also stands alone. For those who have not read the other Mars/Venus books or listened to the tapes, these inspirations will not only be helpful but will serve as an excellent introduction to the simple and basic ideas that have helped millions of individuals and couples.

As you grow in this understanding and insight, you will be better equipped to deal with the inevitable conflicts and challenges that arise in relationships. This does not mean that as you make progress problems will go away. It means that instead of gradually closing your heart and giving up, you will be able to deal with problems in such a way that your heart and love become stronger.

***It is in overcoming love's challenges
that we can grow together in love.***

Listen right now, deep in your heart, to your soul's sincere desire to love and be loved. Make a commitment to yourself to read your daily inspiration, and you will eventually reap your reward. Even though you deserve a loving and lasting relationship, it still takes some work. Let these daily inspirations help you create the relationship of your dreams.

Thank you for letting me make a difference in your life, and thank you for taking the time to create more love in this world. May you continue to grow in love and share the light in your heart.

John Gray
August 1998

❧ JANUARY ❧

Resolve, Excel, Desire

*J*anuary is a time of new beginnings, a time to set our intentions with renewed confidence and innocence. It is a chance to start over. With the last year behind us, we can begin once again, fresh and free. We can question every part of our life and recommit ourselves to achieve and fulfill our soul's desire to love and be loved.

January begins with a sense of exhilaration. We are filled with resolve: "This will be my best year. This will be the year that I discover true and lasting love." Or "This will be the year that, together, we will learn to strengthen our relationship."

The excitement of a new year fills us with a desire to excel. We resolve to take time to consider our own feelings. We try to listen with clarity to our loved ones. We seek the knowledge of what pulls us together. We strive to create deeper and stronger bonds between us.

Yet we know that we will be presented with numerous challenges throughout the year. When these challenges arise, we should keep in mind that a relationship is like a garden: it must be cared for faithfully each day. To tend our garden successfully, we must consider over and over again the unique needs of each of our plants.

A relationship is like a garden:
it must be cared for faithfully each day.

Likewise in our relationships, we need to remember that our partner's needs are often different from ours. Just remembering that men are from Mars and women are from Venus will help you recognize our important differences. With a greater understanding of our differences, we are free to create harmony instead of conflict and realize our sincere desire to make love and be happy together.

Every one of us can create the loving relationship we want, need, and deserve. If you believe that love exists for you, you'll find the power to manifest your dreams. With an open heart, you are able to act in accordance with your highest purpose: to love and be loved.

JANUARY 1

The Seasons of Love

A relationship is like a garden. If it is to thrive, it must be watered regularly. Special care must be given according to the season as well as any unpredictable weather. New seeds must be sown and weeds must be pulled. Similarly, to keep the magic of love alive, we must understand its seasons and nurture love's special needs.

To be successful in our relationships we must accept and understand the different seasons of love. Sometimes love flows easily and automatically; at other times it requires effort. Sometimes our hearts are full, and at other times we are empty. We must not expect our partners always to be loving or even to remember how to be loving. We must also give ourselves this gift of understanding and not expect to remember everything we have learned about being loving. The process of learning requires not only hearing and applying but also forgetting and then remembering again.

Next time you are frustrated with the opposite sex, remember that men are from Mars and women are from Venus. Even if you don't remember anything else, remembering that we are *supposed* to be different will help you be more loving. By gradually releasing your judgments and blame and persistently asking for what you want, you can create the loving relationships you need and deserve.

JANUARY 2

Realizing the Potential of a Relationship

Correctly understanding the way men and women think and feel differently doesn't ensure that a relationship will be free of problems. But it does assist us in lovingly finding a solution.

When we are not getting what we need, we become overly judgmental and critical of our partners. Instead of dwelling on feelings of rejection and resentment we need to focus on getting what we need.

Whenever we are blaming our partner, it is a sign to back off and release our dependence on our partner. By temporarily filling up with love from friends, family, and ourselves, we will be less critical and judgmental. Our judgments and criticisms push away our partner's love. By being more autonomous, we can create a lasting, loving relationship. When we become too dependent, even a soul mate will seem like the wrong partner.

JANUARY 3

Creating Relationships That Support Personal Fulfillment

Women today no longer primarily need men to provide and protect on a physical level. They want men to provide on an emotional level as well. Men today also want more than home-makers and mothers for their children. They want women to nurture their emotional needs, but not to mother them or to treat them like children.

I'm not saying that our parents didn't want emotional support; it was just not their primary expectation. It was enough for Mom if Dad worked and provided. It was enough for Dad if Mom managed the house and kids and didn't constantly nag him.

What was good enough for our parents isn't good enough for us. We are no longer willing to make such enormous personal sacrifices. We demand and deserve lasting happiness, intimacy, and passion with a single partner. If we don't get it, many are prepared to sacrifice the marriage. Personal fulfillment has become more important than the family unit.

There is nothing bad or narcissistic about wanting more than our parents did. The truth is that times have changed, and our values have changed with them.

In most cases, the solution is not divorce nor is it self-sacrifice. Instead, the answer lies in learning how to create relationships and marriages that support our personal fulfillment.

People today are not less loving. Instead, they seek to give and receive even more love.

Until we learn new skills for creating lasting romance, relationships will be disappointing and divorce rates will remain high.

JANUARY 4

⊰⊱

Keeping Love Fresh

Over time in a relationship, we often begin to take our partner for granted. Men stop planning dates and giving them compliments while women stop acknowledging and appreciating the little things a man does to make her life easier. After the honeymoon is over it is too easy to assume that our partner will automatically feel loved and supported. We stop planning ways to express our caring and appreciation.

To overcome this tendency, a wise woman remembers to express her delight whenever possible to a man's attempts to please her. She doesn't dwell on his mistakes but focuses on appreciating his intention to be supportive. Likewise, a wise man remembers to do the little things that say she is special. By thinking ahead in consideration of her needs and wishes and occasionally planning dates and romantic getaways he provides for her the support she needs to feel loved.

~~~~~

Building a Relationship

*T*here are four keys to creating mutually supportive and rewarding relationships:

1. *Purposeful communication*—communicating with the intent to understand and be understood.

2. *Right understanding*—understanding, appreciating, and respecting our differences.

3. *Giving up judgments*—releasing negative judgments of ourselves and others.

4. *Accepting responsibility*—taking equal responsibility for what you get from the relationship and practicing forgiveness.

These four keys can unlock the potential within you to create loving relationships and fulfill your hopes and dreams. They will help you realize why your relationships have had problems in the past, and provide a foundation to build stable and life-enriching relationships in the future.

～⁙～

The Wisdom of Pausing and Preparing

*O*ften a man is offering solutions and a woman wants just to be heard. With advanced relationship skills, a woman can assist him in giving her the support she wants. By learning how to pause and then prepare him to listen, she can continue without getting interrupted by his solution.

The sooner a woman makes it clear that she doesn't need a solution, the easier it will be for her mate to shift gears from the "fixing" mode to the "hearing" mode.

For example, if a man has been listening and begins offering solutions, the woman can pause and let him know that she doesn't need his solutions. It is as simple as saying, "Thanks for the advice but I just need to get this out. You really don't have to say anything." When she is done, she should remember to thank him for listening. For example, she could say, "I feel so much better now, thanks for listening." Or if it was a difficult conversation and things are still unresolved, she could say, "I know this is difficult, but I really appreciate your taking the time to understand my point of view. It helps."

January 7

Why Women Relish Desire

*T*he more a woman is focused throughout her day on caring for and giving to others, the less aware she is of herself and her own sensual desires. She may be in touch with other people's feelings but out of touch with her own.

Just as a man forgets feelings, a woman forgets her sensual desires and longings. The practicalities of day-to-day survival and living take precedence over her deeper and more sensual desires. The more pressured or overwhelmed she is, the harder it is for her to relax and enjoy life's simple pleasures.

> *For a man, the sexual experience is the fulfillment of his desire; for a woman, it is the buildup and then the release.*

When a man focuses on a woman in a caring and attentive way, he frees her to experience herself again. When a woman feels temporarily relieved of her pressure to care for others, she can begin to feel her sexual desires. A man's romantic attention to details designed to please her automatically begins to open her up.

By receiving the caring, nurturing, and sensuous support her female side craves, she begins to feel her sexual yearnings. Sometimes it is as though she doesn't even know she wants this stimulation until she gets it. The act of skillfully giving a woman what she needs helps her to discover her needs, and then she begins to long for more.

January 8

Is There a Part of You That Wants to Have Sex?

*W*hen a man's partner seems uncertain about having sex, instead of giving up, he should say, "Is there a part of you that wants to have sex with me?"

Almost always she will say yes. He may be surprised sometimes by how quickly she will respond by saying, "Sure, a part of me always wants to have sex with you." This will be music to his ears.

She may then proceed to talk about all the reasons she doesn't want to have sex. She might say, "I don't know if we have enough time. I still have to do laundry and some errands." Or she might say, "I'm not sure how I am feeling. I have so much on my mind right now. I feel like I should devote time to finishing this project."

**When a woman seems uncertain about sex,
it doesn't mean no.**

As she continues to talk, he should remind himself that she is not saying no. She just needs to talk, verbally sort things out, and then she can find her desire. Many times after sharing several reasons why she is not in the mood, she will then turn around and say, "Let's do it."

Without understanding how a woman is different, a man can easily feel turned off when she is talking about the reasons she doesn't know if she wants to have sex. As long as he hears that a part of her wants to have sex, it is much easier for him to hear about the parts of her that don't want to have sex. Even if she finally discovers that she doesn't want sex, she can say, "We could have a quickie if you want, and then sometime soon we can be more leisurely about it."

JANUARY 9

How We Stop Loving

*W*hen we feel blame toward our partner, it is difficult to accept, understand, and forgive their limitations and imperfections. Only through learning to love them in stormy times can we grow together. Anybody could love someone who was perfect.

Whenever we are pointing our finger at our partner, three fingers point back.

At times when we are blaming our partner, we need also to look inside, listen to our feelings, and reflect on how we contributed to the problems. We cannot expect our partners to hear our feelings until we can come from a loving, forgiving place.

The test of love is caring for a person even though we know them to be less than perfect and have experienced their daily limitations. We claim that we want to be loved for who we are. But can we really love our partners for who *they* are? Learning to really love is a gradual process requiring both patience and learning to communicate in a loving and non-blaming manner.

꩜

A Man's Responsibility

*F*or a man to enjoy a good relationship with a woman, he must adjust his expectations. Instead of thinking his work is over when he comes home, he must realize that having a relationship is also a part of his work. There will always be obstacles to overcome in sustaining a loving relationship. Too often men assume that once they are married, the work of having a relationship is over.

> ***A great relationship requires a balance of***
> ***work and play.***

A wise man consciously works at the relationship, which helps his partner relax and enjoy more. This makes them both happier. A successful relationship is a balanced mixture of work, play, alone time, and together time.

A man's major responsibility is to counteract his tendency to be overly focused and strive to be caring, respectful, and committed to understanding his partner's feelings and needs, while maintaining his masculine sense of self. By gradually learning to hear her feelings, he will become more motivated to support her and will become aware of his own needs in the relationship. As he puts forth a deliberate effort, she is able to relax more.

The Ebb and Flow of Passion

*I*t is healthy and natural that the wave of passion in a relationship should rise and fall. Just as it is normal not to feel in love with your partner at times, it is also normal not to feel sexually attracted to your partner.

Times when you don't feel sexual attraction are like cloudy days when the sun doesn't shine.

A cloudy day does not mean the sun is not there. It just means that it is temporarily covered. Cloudy days are the times when temptation knocks on our doors. When attraction is blocked in a relationship, many times we feel attracted elsewhere.

At such times it is best not to worry. Rather than feeling frustration, take matters into your own hands. Satisfying yourself sexually is the basis of a healthy sex life. Becoming too dependent on our partner can eventually stifle sexual attraction. To fuel a great sex life, it is important occasionally to satisfy our needs without depending on our partner.

※

What to Do When a Man Is Upset

*W*hile women process their feelings directly through talking, men need to do something while silently thinking about their feelings. Only after first thinking about his feelings will it benefit a man to talk about his feelings.

Generally speaking, a man feels the need to talk mainly when he thinks it will help convey information to solve a problem. If someone has offended or hurt him, he may feel the urge to talk to convey what was wrong or what should change.

A man greatly misunderstands when a woman who is upset wants to talk about it, because he mistakenly believes that she is saying he is wrong and should change. Why? Because when an emotional man feels the same need, he is blaming and accusing. Men must learn that when a woman shares feelings, no matter how angry and accusing she sounds, she is really asking for empathy.

With this new understanding, a woman can appreciate the wisdom of not persisting in trying to draw a man out when he is angry or doesn't want to talk. Not only should she not question him, she should take special pains to postpone conversation gracefully, even if he is willing to talk while emotionally upset.

When a man gets angry, a discussion quickly escalates into a painful agument.

It is helpful to assist a woman in expressing angry feelings if a man can listen without getting angry back. Yet it is not helpful to assist a man in getting his anger out. Instead, give him time to cool off. Watch TV or go to a movie. After pulling away, he will then be able to have a more compassionate discussion.

JANUARY 13

Falling in Love Right Away

*S*ometimes a woman will see something or even imagine something about a man that triggers a surge of confidence in her. She feels, "This is the man of my dreams; he is the one for me; he is perfect for me." It is as though she falls under a spell. In this state, she responds to him as if she were already getting everything she could ever want. She is lovingly responsive and receptive to whatever he does. The excitement certainly brings out the best in her and makes her very attractive, but it can also prevent him from continuing to feel a strong attraction for her.

She feels so satisfied by his presence that she begins to think, "He is so wonderful, what can I do to be worthy of him? How can I make sure he likes me? How can I be most attractive to him?" These kinds of thoughts then lead to action. As she proceeds to pursue him, he becomes less interested in her.

A wise woman is careful to not pursue a man more than he is pursuing her.

A wise woman approaches the situation differently. Even if she does fall in love, she is careful to remember that even though it feels as if she is in an exclusive relationship with her ideal partner, she is not. Even if he has the potential to be the man of her dreams, he is not yet. She needs to remember that they are in stage one. He is not even exclusive with her, nor does she really know him, and they definitely are not engaged to be married. It is vitally important for a woman to remember what stage their relationship is in and respond appropriately to that stage. Having a clear awareness of the stages of dating helps us to keep this balanced perspective. Even in an exclusive relationship a woman needs to practice not giving more or she will inevitably get less.

JANUARY 14

Love and Hate

To love a person doesn't mean we will always agree with them or even feel good about them. It doesn't mean we will like all of the things they do or don't do. Nobody is perfect. Whenever you like a person, there will always be some things you dislike too. And if you really love someone, it inevitably happens that sometimes you not only dislike what they do but you hate it. For most people, "hate" is a dirty word. It's thought to be taboo to feel hate toward your partner. That's only allowed during divorce proceedings!

Hate is really just a symptom of obstructed love. When you love someone who does something that is hard for you to love and accept, for some the natural reaction is to hate that behavior. And you want to change the person so that you can love them again.

All suppressed resentment culminates in hate. If you don't give yourself permission to feel hate sometimes, it gets repressed, and along with it you repress your ability to love fully.

Feeling hate is a sign that your feelings are blocked. Dwelling on feelings of hate is not useful, but being aware of it can point the way to releasing our blocks to loving. Underlying hate are always feelings of anger, sadness, fear, and sorrow. By looking a little deeper than the surface feeling of hate and exploring the four healing emotions, you can once again feel your feelings of love.

Unresolved anger and resentment gradually turn to hate.

When you can't share and express your negative feelings, they build up and get blown out of proportion. Or you may work very hard at repressing them and think they are forgotten. They may be forgotten, but they still have an effect—you are cursed to overreact emotionally in your relationships or push others away with hate.

It Sounds Worse Than It Is

*W*hen a woman shows feelings, a man tends to minimize them. He thinks he is helping her to feel better. Men often say things to each other like "Don't worry about it" or "It's not such a big deal." Though this may work on Mars, it doesn't work on Venus.

> **Most men don't instinctively realize that by just listening to a woman's upset feelings, they will automatically become more positive, accepting, and trusting.**

A wise woman realizes that a man will make her feelings much more important if she doesn't demand it. Instead of minimizing her feelings, he will relax and listen. Preparing a man by saying "It's not really a big deal. I just want you to consider how I feel" will enable him to listen much more attentively than before.

At other times, when a woman wants to initiate conversation, a good technique to use to prepare the man to listen is to say, "I have a lot of feelings coming up, and I would like to talk about them. I just want you to know in advance that it sounds worse than it is. I just need to talk for a while and feel that you care. You don't have to say anything or do anything differently." This kind of approach will help him to listen with empathy rather than try to figure out what to do.

JANUARY 16

Breaking Up with Love

Many times when we want to leave a person, we start gathering evidence to justify saying good-bye. We start keeping a mental list of all our partner's "crimes," and then one day we spring it on them: "Here is the evidence. You are bad. I have been abused, and so I have a reason to leave."

Before ending a relationship, it is important to resolve the buildup of negative emotions toward your partner and to feel the love and gratitude again. When the love in a relationship gets repressed due to a continued lack of communication, you are bound to feel less love for your partner. Just as you cannot tell if you are right for each other without love, so you cannot tell if you are wrong for each other without feeling the love and seeing the reasons why you got together in the first place.

You do not have to stop loving your partner to leave them. If you are honest with yourself and have resolved your resentments toward your partner, you will always feel love toward them. Breaking up with love helps prepare us to find love once again.

Just as an open heart reveals the right person, it also reveals the wrong person for us.

Some relationships are right for us to learn certain lessons or to grow in a particular way. These relationships prepare us to find the right person to share our life with. In a growth relationship, our partner is right to help us take a step of growth, and then we are ready to move on. This insight helps us to move on without having to build up a case against our partner. Loving someone doesn't mean we must spend the rest of our lives with them.

JANUARY 17

Why Couples Are Having Less Sex

*C*ouples today are having much less sex than the media suggest. Yes, a lot of hungry men and women are out there wanting sex, but once they are married a few years, other things become more important, and sex is overlooked.

The primary reason for this loss of interest is that men feel rejected and women don't feel romanced and understood in the relationship. A woman does not instinctively realize how sensitive a man is when she isn't in the mood for sex. A man does not instinctively realize how much a woman needs romance and good communication to open up and feel in the mood.

For men not to feel rejected, couples need to create free, positive, and easy communication about sex, particularly about initiating sex. When a man repeatedly gets the message that his partner loves sex with him, his sexual desires can remain healthy and strong.

When a woman feels that a man is skilled in sex, and he supports her in the relationship, her sexual desire can remain fresh. Good communication and loving support in the relationship are most important for a woman. For a man, a good relationship is certainly important, but many times what makes the big difference is his sexual success with her.

When sex diminishes, most couples don't realize there is a problem.

When couples stop having sex several times a week, rather than assuming they are just not interested anymore, they need to recognize that they are blocked. An important part of a healthy relationship is regular sex, two or three times a week. Less sex means that you could benefit greatly from sex therapy, sexy movies, and reading sex manuals together.

"Use it or lose it" most aptly describes a lasting sex life.

If you want a healthy body over the age of forty, you need to exercise. Likewise, if you want to keep the fires of passion, you have to keep having frequent sex. Women don't realize how important sex is to men. If they don't get it, men gradually lose interest and sexual vitality. Fortunately, with therapy it can be awakened once again.

⋙⋘

Personal Responsibility and Self-Healing

*A*s we continue to open up and have our emotional needs met in a relationship, our unresolved past feelings ultimately begin to surface. When they rise up, they don't say, "Hi, I'm your anger with your dad"; instead they are directed at our partners.

It is ironic that when we feel most loved, the unresolved feelings from past experiences of not being loved begin to affect our moods. One minute we are feeling passion, the next we are considering divorce. We always justify such radical shifts by our partner's behavior, although it really isn't primarily about them.

> **Blaming your partner is looking in the wrong direction and aggravates the wound.**

When past feelings begin to surface, they generally make us feel uncharacteristically negative. We may feel a lot of blame, criticism, doubt, resentment, confusion, ambivalence, judgment, and rejection. For a moment, we regress to feeling and reacting the way we did as children, when we didn't feel safe to react freely. When such feelings surface, it is vital for us to work on taking responsibility for being more loving and forgiving.

We should not expect our partners to be our loving parents. That, as we know, is a surefire passion killer. At those times, we need to parent ourselves, or work with a surrogate parent therapist in counseling. It is up to us, not our partners, to reparent ourselves.

When we start blaming our partners for our unhappiness, it is a clear signal that our own "old stuff" is coming up. Although we feel especially entitled to demand more from our mates, we should demand nothing. It is a time for self-healing. It is a time for us to give ourselves the comfort and understanding our parents may have failed to give us.

Remember, to expect our partners to make us feel better is to put them in the role of parents. The more dependent we become on them to change before we can change, the more stuck we will be. By parenting ourselves, we are free to release them from being the targets of our blame.

JANUARY 19

Change Is Hard Work

*C*hanging for the better is sometimes hard work, but at each progressive step it will also become easier, more rewarding, and more fun. Once learned, these skills will enrich all aspects of your life and relationships.

The most important relationship skill of all is anticipating temporary setbacks and acknowledging the necessity of relearning a lesson until it becomes second nature. This understanding gives us the hope to be patient and the forgiveness to be loving.

Although learning new skills may seem overwhelming at times, the process is also very exciting. As you begin to practice new relationship skills, the immediate and tangible results will give you continued cause for hope, encouragement, and support.

With your very first step on this journey, your relationships can dramatically and immediately improve, and with more practice, they will keep on getting better.

By learning these essential skills, you can achieve lasting passion, intimacy, and happiness. Passion does not have to dissipate. The happiness shared during the courting process does not have to fade. Intimacy can deepen into a source of increasing fulfillment.

JANUARY 20

Relearning Love

*I*t's easy to fall in love, but it's a lot harder to stay in love. We all want love to last. We all want to live happily ever after. No one decides to get married and says to their partner, "Hey, Honey, I've been thinking. Let's get married and have a wonderful two or three years together. Then let's get tired of each other and get divorced—what do you say?" or "Darling, let's live together and have a great sex life for five years, then let's start fighting, feel resentful, have some extramarital affairs, and then split up." No one falls in love and plans to fall out of love. But it happens, and when it happens, it hurts.

If you want a relationship that is better than the one your parents had, if you want love to work for you, you have to work at it. Start by admitting to yourself that you need to learn how to make love work. Let go of your pride and feel the need you have deep inside for more intimacy, appreciation, and love. The easiest way to learn is to pretend that you don't know anything about love. Try adopting beginner's awareness as you take this next step.

Beginner's awareness opens up the door to learning something new.

Enriching your relationships is an art and a science, just like building a bridge, making a meal, or playing an instrument. It takes skills and practice through daily application of those skills. Enriching your relationship will seem like a mystery, like something impossible to comprehend, until you have worked with it long enough to master it. Then it will be second nature.

Regardless of your past history, enriching your relationship can be learned.

JANUARY 21

The Wisdom of Waiting

*T*he wisdom of waiting to be fully intimate is that a man's desire has a chance to grow into higher levels of expression. When a man takes time to move through the first three stages of dating (attraction, uncertainty, and exclusivity), his physical desire expands into the emotional desire to please the woman. His desire to please her in turn develops into a genuine interest in who she is. This interest in who she is then has a chance to turn into love. When his physical desire is also the expression of his love for a woman, this is the best time to experience increasing degrees of intimacy.

Waiting to be intimate can take a variety of forms. You may choose to be sexual right away but hold back from revealing all of who you are emotionally. Or you may choose to restrain the urge to have sex until you get to know a person emotionally and mentally. By wisely holding back from sharing all of yourself on the first date, you create an opportunity for interest and curiosity to grow.

Every relationship is unique. When it comes to answering the question "How long should I wait?" listen to your heart. Women must be careful not to assume that a man is exclusive or committed if they have sex.

Often women start on a date to explore the relationship and *then* choose whether they want to have sex. In an opposite manner, men first seek sex and then choose whether they want a relationship. Waiting to have sex does not in any way ensure a man's desire. Nor does having sex right way prevent a man from being more interested. But if a woman has sex to "get a man," this may push him away. To sustain a positive view of men, a woman needs to recognize that just as she is free to choose when to have sex, he is free to choose when he wants a relationship after sex. When a man is frustrated that a woman doesn't want to have sex, she is not to be blamed. Likewise, when a man has sex and then doesn't want a relationship, he is not to be blamed.

Having an exclusive relationship provides the foundation for lasting intimacy. A woman creates intimacy by honestly sharing more of who she is, and a man experiences increased intimacy by successfully supporting and nurturing more of who she is as well as by sharing himself. As she discloses herself more, he can gradually get to know her. If he continues to be supportive as he gets to know her better, the love he feels in his heart has a chance to grow.

~≈≈≈~

Releasing Negative Feelings

*I*t is not very difficult to release negative feelings, but it takes a deliberate intention and an understanding of how to do it. Most people are not taught how. The secret is to talk about what is bothering you to someone. By telling the complete truth about your feelings, the negative feelings can be released and positive feelings come back.

Yet this doesn't always work. We may talk about our feelings and just feel stuck in them. When this is the case, it is generally because we are overlooking a feeling. We may be angry or sad, but we are not aware of our fears. We can be assured of moving through our negative feelings when we take the time to explore all of the four healing feelings: anger, sadness, fear, and regret. Each of the four feelings is equally important. When we are ignoring one of the four feelings, it may cause us to remain stuck in the others.

> **Talking about our feelings doesn't always work;**
> **it may cause us to feel even more stuck.**

Taking time to explore these feelings releases you once again to feel your positive desire to love and be loved. This positive attitude awakens within you the necessary resources to resolve life's upsets and problems—such resources as patience, persistence, hope, understanding, acceptance, compassion, generosity, calmness, appreciation, respect, trust, forgiveness, and caring.

When the setting is right, talking about these feelings is sometimes the most effective way to release them. But sometimes talking can prevent us from exploring each of the four levels. The presence and response of another person can inhibit the expression of certain feelings.

We may not want to be fully honest because we do not want to sound too negative or because we may get a negative response. For example, if you were to become angry, your partner might become angry back. Getting angry back and forth makes it even more difficult for you to let go of negative feelings and to find love and forgiveness. When the listener responds defensively with anger, we become stuck at the level of anger instead of moving from anger to sadness, fear, sorrow, and love.

With this insight, the solution becomes simple but powerful. Whenever you begin to notice your resentment, sit down and write a Feeling Letter to your partner. Express all your anger and resentment, moving down through your sadness, fear, and regret. Miraculously, a new rush of love will bubble up, and you will be genuinely able to forgive your partner and be in love again. Then, from a more loving place, you can talk to your partner about your wishes, feelings, and needs.

Writing a Feeling Letter frees you to find your positive feelings again without depending so much on your partner. Some people resist this process of self-exploration, claiming that they don't want to write out their feelings, but demand that their partner listen. This is an unrealistic expectation and puts an unhealthy burden on the partner and the relationship.

It is unfair to expect our partner to hear our feelings if we will not take the time to hear our feelings first. Taking time to write out your negative feelings will free you to be more positive when you eventually share your more resolved feelings and wishes with your partner. When we come from a more loving, forgiving, and open place, it is much easier for others to hear us and respond in the ways we hope for.

> *It is unfair to expect our partner to hear our feelings if we will not take the time to hear our feelings first.*

To be open and forgiving doesn't mean that you agree with your partner's behavior. To forgive is to resolve your emotional resistance so that your love can flow as freely as it did before. To forgive is to give your love as before. Forgiveness releases your partner from being responsible for your feelings and affirms that you are once again responsible for feeling better again. To write out your feelings is a deliberate step in taking the responsibility to release your negative feelings and paves the way to open and forgiving communication.

What Men Really Want

*W*hat a man really wants in a relationship is to feel successful in making his partner happy. Her fulfillment not only makes him happier but lightens his load. Her happiness signals to him that he is loved. Her warm responses are like a mirror reflecting back to him a shining image.

With increasing stress in our lives, this goal becomes more difficult to achieve. When a man gets home, often his wife is not only overwhelmed but exhausted. Instead of feeling confident in his ability to make her happy, he becomes frustrated and may eventually sink into apathy. He begins to feel that he can't make her happy.

> *A woman's warm responses and expression of appreciation*
> *are like a mirror reflecting back to him*
> *a shining image.*

Deep in his soul, a man hopes his partner will acknowledge and appreciate his efforts and in some measure be fulfilled by them. When she does not seem happy to see him, something very significant begins to happen. His tender but passionate desire to please her, protect her, and provide for her is dampened and is eventually snuffed out.

Men don't generally pinpoint what is happening inside themselves because they are more concerned with trying to figure out how to make women happy. Yet the more a woman acts and reacts from feelings of unhappiness, something inside a man switches off. When his hard work seems to count for nothing, his life and relationship lose all magic and meaning for him.

With this insight, a woman is naturally more motivated to let a man know when she is happy. Regular acknowledgment and appreciation helps a man remember that he is successful, even though sometimes she is overwhelmed and exhausted. In this way, a woman can confidently and deliberately give her partner what he wants most.

January 24

Women Love Sex

Women love sex, but before they can feel their desire for it, they have more requirements than men do. A man doesn't readily understand this because throughout his life he gets many messages that women don't like sex. To sustain passion and attraction in a relationship over the years, a man needs clear messages that a woman loves sex with him.

As a general rule, men peak in their sexual interest when they are seventeen or eighteen years old. A woman reaches her prime when she is thirty-six to thirty-eight years old. It is similar to the pattern that men and women experience during sex. The man gets excited very quickly with little foreplay—except the opportunity to have sex—while a woman requires more time. Quite naturally, he may begin to feel that she doesn't like sex as much as he does.

> *A man mistakenly concludes that a woman doesn't want*
> *or need sex, because she has more requirements than he does.*

His mother's attitude about sex may also influence him. If, as an adolescent, he was afraid of having his mother find out about his growing interest in sex and girls, he might have gotten the message that it is not okay to want sex. Later in life, when he is with a woman that he cares about, these subconscious feelings can begin to emerge as little voices or faint feelings saying "I can't be sexual around her, or I will be rejected."

These past experiences may not directly cause a man to lose interest, but they certainly make him more sensitive to feeling rejected when a woman seems uninterested in sex. When she is not in the mood, subconsciously he begins to feel, "I knew it. She doesn't want to have sex."

One of the ways to counteract this tendency is for a woman to give the man repeated subtle messages that she likes sex. Her acceptance of occasional quickies is the strongest message of support she can give. Another powerfully positive message is to be very supportive whenever he initiates sex.

Avoiding Painful Arguments

*W*hen a woman is emotionally upset but denies or suppresses her feelings in an attempt to be logical and rational, she is bound to experience many arguments. At such times, her statements will be rigid and opinionated. This is not only offensive to a man but threatening. It tells him there is no room for his ideas to be true and that his differing points of view are not being appreciated. While she thinks she is making sense to him, he becomes angry and dumps out his negative emotions.

On the other hand, if a man just dumps out his negative feelings without considering his partner's point of view objectively, he can create serious defensiveness in her. Here again, she will tend to be opinionated and rigid. From this perspective, arguments are a no-win situation and should be avoided.

To avoid painful arguments, stop talking and take a time-out as soon as you begin to feel defensive, hurt, or argumentative.

It is hard enough to resolve our differences when we are feeling loving and supportive. If negative emotions come up in an argument, it is time to cool off before resuming. Arguing is inevitable, but at least we can do it respectfully and with a lot of understanding.

When we begin hurting each other, it is time to slow down, take a time-out, and come back later to resolve the issue.

Both men and women are vulnerable to arguments, but they are unaware of the injurious effect they have on each other when they argue. The impact of arguments should not be taken lightly. Although the parties are not physically damaging each other, on a psychological level they are creating bruises that will take time to heal. The closer we are to someone, the easier it is to bruise or be bruised.

JANUARY 26

Chemistry Is Not Created

*C*hemistry on any level cannot be created. You cannot make someone physically attracted to you. All you can do is create the right conditions for that person to discover what chemistry is possible. You cannot drill a well just anywhere and expect to find water.

When a woman in a restaurant gets up and walks to the rest room, a man gets to see her. Either he feels the chemistry or he doesn't. The same woman viewed by different men will evoke different degrees of attraction and interest.

With good communication and quality time,
we can create the conditions for chemistry to be felt.

In other words, we cannot create emotional, mental, or spiritual chemistry. It just is. What we can do is create the right conditions for people to discover how much they love us, or how much they find us truly interesting, or how much they want to make us happy. All we can do is make sure they have the opportunity to feel chemistry to the degree that it exists.

By setting up the right conditions in the earlier stages, we give whatever chemistry is potentially there a chance to be felt. When you have seen the best of a person over time, then your heart has a chance to open. With enough love in your heart, you are then prepared to experience the worst of that person and still come back to a loving connection. You are able to hold them in your heart even though you may be frustrated or disappointed. This is real love.

JANUARY 27

What Do You Say When a Man Is Upset?

If a man is upset and wants to talk, a woman tends to assume that he will calm down through talking. This is only true if she agrees with what he says. In most cases when a man is upset, the more you get him to talk the worse things become. By understanding that men are from Mars, a woman can remember that talking it out is not always the best solution.

> ***When a man is angry or resentful,***
> ***this is not the time to draw him out through conversation.***

Commonly a woman would not consider keeping a man from sharing his feelings, because she would not want him to do that to her. If she were upset, she would want him to listen. Instinctively, she knows that if she has a chance to share her feelings, she will feel better. She needs someone to listen but does not require that he agree.

Men are different. When they are upset, they have a much greater need to be right. If they remain quiet for a while, they automatically take time to reflect on the situation and cool off. If a woman feels she can't agree with or at least appreciate his points when he is angry, then, although it may seem rude, she must postpone the conversation. She could say, "I understand you are upset. Let me think about this and then we can talk later."

How she handles the postponement is very important. She should not be accusatory because that will only inflame him. What she should do is briefly validate his feelings and then postpone discussion. Without saying anything else, she should walk away as if what she is doing is perfectly normal and everything is fine. This is a new relationship skill, which allows him to save face and cool off.

JANUARY 28

❧❧❧

Share and Share Alike

*M*en commonly expect there to be no more problems once they are in a relationship, and women expect a man to fulfill their needs without having to be reminded again and again. When these mistaken assumptions are corrected, communication improves. He can more easily hear about problems, and she can share her needs in a more supportive way. With better communication, they are then able to share more equally the burdens—and the joys—of the relationship.

A man needs to remember that a relationship is similar to his work. It would be unrealistic to think that everything should be easy and fun. Any great achievement always requires persistence, patience, problem-solving, and hard work. Blood, sweat, and tears are required not only at work but also at home. If we are to create loving, passionate, and satisfying relationships, we need a balance of work and play. Sometimes relationships are hard work, but if we do the work, then we can relax and enjoy the results of creating better communication and intimacy at other times.

> **Blood, sweat, and tears are required**
> **not only at work but also at home.**

A woman needs to remember that men are from Mars—that they don't instinctively remember a woman's needs and wants or recognize what is important to her. Just as a man must overcome his resistance to working at a relationship, a woman must overcome her resistance to asking gracefully for what she wants. Often she feels that if she has to ask or remind, her partner really doesn't love her. With this insight, she can resolve to ask for what she wants without the expectation that he should already know or always remember.

January 29

~~~

Keeping the Magic of Romance Alive

*W*hile men hunger for great sex, women long for romance. Even the tough-minded, goal-oriented, high-powered executive woman places great value on romance. Romance has a magical effect on women everywhere.

Women spend billions of dollars each year on romance novels. To fulfill a woman's need for romance, a man first needs to understand what romance is.

Receiving cards, cut flowers, and little presents; moonlit nights; spontaneous decisions as well as planned dates; and eating out all spell romance for a woman.

It is not that men are unwilling to create romance. A man just doesn't get why it is so important. In the beginning he is happy to be romantic to show her how special she is, but once he has behaved romantically, he doesn't instinctively realize why he has to keep doing it. If he had repeatedly witnessed his father being romantic to his mother, it probably wouldn't have to be a learned skill. Taking time to create romance is essential if we are to expect romance to last.

JANUARY 30

Equal Partnership Creates Lasting Passion

*W*hile equal partnership is the secret of success in a relationship, it can also be an obstacle. To create lasting passion in a relationship, it is helpful to understand how men and women experience partnership differently. By making sure men and women get their needs met, an equal partnership ensures a lifetime of love.

A woman instinctively feels partnership when she and her partner are doing things together in a cooperative manner toward the same goal. There is no hierarchy or boss. They make all decisions together, sharing their input equally. This intimate cooperation gives a woman the feeling of equal participation.

A man experiences partnership differently. He likes to have his department, where he is in control, and he is happy for her to have her department, where she is in control. He doesn't want her telling him what to do, nor does he feel he has to be involved with what she is doing. Together, doing different jobs with different responsibilities, they are a partnership teaming up to get the job done. In this different manner, he feels they are cooperating to achieve a common goal.

Although men and women experience partnership differently, a healthy compromise can be found.

With an awareness of this difference, men and women can create the partnership they want. The secret of success is in having both kinds of partnership. Sometimes they do things separately, and at other times they work together. When working together, the woman must be careful to appreciate what the man contributes, and when working apart, the man must be careful to respect the woman's wishes and needs.

In addition, for a partnership to thrive, it must not be just self-serving; it must have a purpose beyond itself. For the passion to grow, partners eventually must share a common interest and work toward some end or cause outside their own personal needs.

JANUARY 31

<center>~~~~~</center>

A Man's Purpose in a Relationship

*I*n a relationship, a man's purpose is to provide support for the woman and receive her love in return. As long as he stays "on purpose," a relationship has a chance to grow. When he starts to focus only on what he is getting in return, he gets "off purpose" and the woman begins to close down.

Romantic rituals help a man to stay on purpose. In most of the traditional romantic rituals, the man provides and the woman graciously receives. These rituals are important because they give him the repeated experience that he can succeed in his purpose very easily. All he has to do is plan a date, make a few calls, spend a little money, open doors, and he is suddenly a great guy. She appreciates him, and he feels good.

Romantic rituals are important because they give a man the repeated experience of success.

When a woman graciously receives his support without feeling obligated to give in return, it uplifts her as well. Romantic rituals are there to make her feel special and to remind her to receive and not give so much. In this process, he gets the opportunity once again to taste the nectar of being selfless and giving unconditionally.

❧ FEBRUARY ❧

Understand, Embrace, Commit

February is a month in which we find ourselves fully immersed in winter's powerful grip. It is a time that holds the faintest hope of a spring to come, while often challenging us with the most powerful forces of nature.

Our emotions challenge us at this time as well. We must work hard to understand each other, so that we can learn to love and embrace our differences. We must commit, again and again, to the art of patience and sharing.

This is a time of year when we frequently see men pull away from the closeness of coupling to rediscover their need for independence and autonomy. When a woman accepts a man's need to pull away, she sets the right conditions for him to rediscover within himself his desire to be close to her.

Women also face emotional challenges. If a woman has

suppressed any negative feelings or denied herself in order to be more loving, she begins to experience the downside of these negative feelings and unfulfilled needs. During this downtime, she especially needs to talk about problems and be understood.

To understand, to embrace, and to commit, we must share in the complex needs of the person we love. Although sometimes this is not easy, the challenges of loving bring out the best in us. This is a month to focus on creating love and romance to counter these natural challenges. With a little extra attention to creating romance, you can avoid difficult times and make the love you share most memorable.

FEBRUARY 1

What Makes Relationships Difficult

*A*t no time in history have relationships been so difficult for men and women. It used to be that a man came home from work not expecting to provide more. Coming home was a time to relax and unwind and not another job. Women likewise experience the pressures of going to work and then coming home and feeling added responsibilities. For both men and women, the home is no longer a place of comfort but often an added burden at the end of the day.

When a man loves a woman, his primary goal is to make her happy. Throughout history, men have endured the competitive and hostile world of work because, at the end of the day, their struggles and efforts were justified by a woman's appreciation. In a very real sense, his mate's fulfillment was the reward that made a man's labor worthwhile. Men could tolerate the stress of the work world because they could relax and feel nurtured at home.

Women are affected more adversely than men by career stress, for the pressures of work outside the home have doubled their load. On the job, women give as much as men do, and when they get home, instinct takes over and they continue giving. Although some men help out at home, it is rarely with anything close to the energy that a woman tends to give.

When women come home,
they too are looking for a wife to greet them
at the door.

For most women, the home awakens a nesting instinct. Even if she wants to rest and relax, she can't until the home is in order. A man is different. Although he may appreciate a neat and tidy home, if he is tired he would rather rest than clean up. In a certain way, men and women have opposite reactions. When tired or exhausted, men tend to care less, while women tend to care more.

The harmful effects of this relatively new pattern are greatly underestimated by women and men. Although I am in no way suggesting that we turn back the clock and encourage women back into the kitchen, it is important that we understand what we have given up. As we stride forward on our quest for a new and better world for women and men, we need to keep in mind the wisdom of the past and use it wherever applicable. Contained in that ancient wisdom are certain elements that are essential for female and male contentment.

We should never lose touch with the ancient truths that have always enhanced female and male fulfillment. By understanding them, we can more effectively map out fresh approaches to relating that fulfill our instincts while allowing us to move ahead to new goals and dreams. It is not how much a woman does or how much a man helps out but the quality of her relationships and the emotional support she receives that determine the difference between burnout and fulfillment for a woman. By recognizing a woman's need to communicate and share her feelings, a man can more successfully support his partner in relaxing.

Likewise, a woman can remember to ask a man for his support gracefully and appreciate his efforts rather than just assuming that he should automatically be motivated to help out. Through good communication and romance, balance can be achieved. When a man begins to experience that helping with the dishes is great foreplay, he gradually has more energy for it.

FEBRUARY 2

Dealing with Doubt

*W*hile dating and even after getting married, it is common to feel uncertain about our partner at times. We wonder if we picked the right person or if we should be married at all. It is not true that if we are with the right person we will always know for sure. Uncertainty is natural, and it usually precedes greater clarity and understanding.

During the courting process, when one person is more special than others, we automatically move into stage two of dating, uncertainty. When we begin to feel that we would really like to get to know that person and have an exclusive relationship, it is quite natural suddenly to shift and not feel so sure. For some, that shift is like an earthquake, and for others, it is a mild tremor. Sometimes the size of the shift or the suddenness with which it occurs is a signal that this person has good potential.

We could be with our soul mate and still feel doubts.

Doubt has less to do with our partner and more to do with our ability to trust ourselves. We could actually be dating our soul mate but not know it. Whether the person is wrong or right, we are all at times subject to feelings of uncertainty. Unfortunately, many singles do not recognize this as a necessary stage and mistakenly assume that if they are not certain, this must not be the right person for them. They think that if they have found the right person, the gates of heaven should open and bells should ring.

In a similar way, couples may panic when feelings of doubt or uncertainty come up. To pave the way for a long-lasting relationship, we must make room for periods of doubt and uncertainty. Love flows in cycles. When we are doubting our relationship, that is generally a time to focus more on loving and supporting ourselves than expecting our partner's support. It is unhealthy to expect our partner always to be there for us.

At those times when we do not feel much support from our partners, we must look to healthy and supportive relationships with friends, family, and God to support us. As we experience this fulfillment without depending on our partner, then quite automatically the wave of uncertainty is replaced by a wave of confidence and attraction for our partner once again.

꧁꧂

Money Can't Buy Love

*T*hough lots of money can buy nice things, it also makes relationships more challenging. Repeatedly I have witnessed couples who love each other on the way up the road to riches but begin to hate each other once they make it. With a greater understanding of our different emotional needs, more money and greater success can instead be a great blessing to a relationship.

Financial success creates problems when couples are not prepared with the necessary relationship skills. As a couple becomes more financially secure, the man mistakenly assumes that the woman will be happier as well. When they were poor, he could understand her occasional periods of unhappiness. As they begin to earn more money and own more things, he can't understand why she continues to have periods of unhappiness and dissatisfaction.

The man mistakenly assumes that when the couple's physical needs can all be met, his job is done, and he can relax. The woman's experience is different. When her physical needs for security and survival are met, she begins to feel her emotional needs more.

When they were poor, it was okay if he was busy working. They needed the money for food. Now that there is food on the table, other things, like talking, communicating, intimacy, and romance, become more important. Suddenly the woman requires more from the relationship.

> *At a time when a man thinks his job is done,*
> *a woman is busy writing a new job description.*

When a relationship undergoes the shift from being physically based to being emotionally oriented, a couple needs to know it is inevitable that new problems will come up. The old ways of relating to each other will not be satisfactory or fulfilling.

Since women are generally more conscious of their emotional needs, the woman is first to experience a lack of fulfillment. Her male partner, in turn, begins to feel a lack of fulfillment in response to the woman's dissatisfaction. As they become more successful, he grows more intolerant of her dissatisfaction. Neither is happy, and each tends to blame the other. One of the biggest problems is that they both resent having these difficulties in the first place.

These new problems cannot be avoided, but they can be solved. If the two understand and accept that this is inevitable, they will not be resentful of each other. They will not question the relationship; instead they will question their old styles of relating and communicating. Rather than changing partners, they can focus their energies on improving their abilities to give and receive emotional support.

The Importance of Timing

*C*ave time for a man is solitary time when he can most effectively recuperate from the day, forget his problems by staring off into the fire, gradually connect with his loving feelings, and remember what is most important to him. Once he feels better, he automatically comes out of the cave and is available for a relationship.

After spending alone time in his cave, a man can release the stress of his day and be ready for a relationship.

To ensure mutually supportive conversations, a woman needs to postpone her immediate needs to share her feelings until her male partner is out of the cave. It is disastrous to initiate a conversation before a man is actually capable of listening and sharing. By pausing in this way and waiting for the right time to share her feelings, a woman can get the support she most needs.

When a man can't take the time he needs for himself, it is extremely difficult for him to find the loving feelings that originally attracted him to his partner. In a similar way, when a woman doesn't get the chance to share her feelings and connect with her female side, she, as well, loses touch with her deep, loving feelings. Just as a woman needs to practice giving a man his cave time, a man needs to practice being attentive to a woman's need to talk about her day.

～✦～

Understanding the Cave

*W*omen have a lot to learn about men before their relationships can be really fulfilling. They need to learn that when a man is upset or stressed, he will automatically stop talking and go to his cave to work things out. They need to learn that no one is allowed in that cave, not even the man's best friends. This was the way it was on Mars. Women should not be afraid that they have done something terribly wrong. They need gradually to learn that if you just let men go into their caves, after a while they will come out and everything will be fine.

This lesson is difficult for women because on Venus, one of the golden rules was never to abandon a friend when she was upset. It just doesn't seem loving to abandon her favorite Martian when he is upset. Since she cares for him, a woman wants to come into his cave and offer him help. This only upsets Martians more. She instinctively wants to support him in the way she would want to be supported. Her intentions are good, but the outcome is counterproductive.

Women mistakenly conclude that by asking a lot of questions and being a good listener, they can help a man feel better.

In a variety of ways, what a woman assumes a man needs is the opposite of what he really needs. Just as a woman feels supported when someone asks interested and caring questions, a man may feel the opposite. Both men and women need to stop offering the method of caring they would prefer and start to learn the different ways their partners think, feel, and react.

FEBRUARY 6

Why Men Pull Away

*W*hen a woman learns the skill of temporarily postponing her needs and allows a man the time he needs to shift gears from his work life to his home life, she creates a fertile ground for him to find his love for her and then act on it. As he grows accustomed to this support, he begins to anticipate it. At this point, just the thought of returning home begins releasing his stress. The more he gets this kind of support, the less he needs to pull away from his mate.

Without this new relationship skill, a woman unknowingly prevents her male partner from successfully making the transition from work to home. If a woman demands more of him or reacts negatively to his need for private time, he may never relax enough to come back into the relationship. If the downward spiral continues, a man can become blocked from contacting his loving feelings. He may even believe that he doesn't love his partner anymore.

The more he feels pressured to talk or be "in relationship," the more he needs to back off to relax. He can most effectively forget the demands of his job when he feels no pressure or demands from his mate.

When a man returns home to a nondemanding woman, he feels free to take the time he needs to relax. He can then automatically shift gears and give his partner the love she deserves. Literally thousands of women who have applied this relationship skill report that this single insight has magically transformed their relationships.

FEBRUARY 7

Men Are Like Rubber Bands

*M*en are like rubber bands. When they pull away, they can stretch only so far before they come springing back. A rubber band is the perfect metaphor to understand the male intimacy cycle. This cycle involves getting close, pulling away, and then getting close again.

Most women are surprised to realize that even when a man loves a woman, periodically he needs to pull away before he can get closer. Men instinctively feel this urge to pull away. It is not a decision or choice. It just happens. It is neither his fault nor her fault. It is a natural cycle.

Women misinterpret a man's pulling away because generally a woman pulls away for different reasons. She pulls back when she doesn't trust a man to understand her feelings, when she has been hurt and is afraid of being hurt again, or when he has done something wrong and disappointed her. Certainly a man may pull away for the same reasons, but he will also pull away even if she has done nothing wrong. He may love and trust her, but then suddenly he will begin to pull away. Like a stretched rubber band, he will distance himself and then come back all on his own.

Distance makes the heart grow stronger.

A man pulls away to fulfill his need for independence or autonomy. When he has fully stretched away, then instantly he will come springing back. When he has fully separated, then he will feel his need for love and intimacy again. Automatically he will be more motivated to give his love and receive the love he needs. When a man springs back, he picks up the relationship at whatever degree of intimacy it was when he stretched away. He doesn't feel any need for a period of getting reacquainted again.

When a woman accepts a man's need to pull away, she sets the right conditions for him to find within himself his desire to be close to her. By supporting a man's tendency to pull away, a woman ensures that he can find the love in his heart to come back.

If a man does not have the opportunity to pull away, he never gets a chance to feel his strong desire to be close. It is essential for women to understand that if they insist on continuous intimacy or run after their intimate male partner when he pulls away, then he will almost always be trying to escape and distance himself. He will never get a chance to feel his own passionate longing for love.

꧁꧂

Women Are Like Waves

A woman is like a wave. When she feels loved, her self-esteem rises and falls in a wave motion. When she is feeling really good, she reaches a peak, but then suddenly her mood may change and her wave crashes down. This crash is temporary. After she reaches bottom, her mood will shift suddenly and she will again feel good about herself. Automatically her wave begins to rise back up.

When a woman's wave rises, she feels she has an abundance of love to give, but when it falls, she feels her inner emptiness and needs to be filled up with love. This time of bottoming out is a time for emotional housecleaning. By recognizing this pattern, a man doesn't take it personally. When he doesn't feel as if he is being blamed for her downs, he can be more supportive.

> *Knowing that a woman's feelings rise and fall like waves*
> *helps a man to be understanding without taking it personally.*

If she has suppressed any negative feelings or denied herself in order to be more loving on the upswing of her wave, she begins to experience these negative feelings and unfulfilled needs on the downswing. During this downtime, she especially needs to talk about problems and be understood.

My wife, Bonnie, says this experience of downtime is like going into a dark well. When a woman goes into her well, she is consciously sinking into her unconscious self, into darkness and diffused feeling. She may suddenly experience a host of unexplained emotions and vague feelings. She may feel hopeless, thinking she is all alone or unsupported. Soon after she reaches the bottom, if she feels loved and supported, she will automatically start to feel better. As suddenly as she may have crashed, she will automatically rise up and again radiate love in her relationships.

FEBRUARY 9

Signals That He Is Out of the Cave

A man can help a woman know when he is out of the cave by giving her clear signals in a language that she will understand. Touching a woman in a nonsexual but affectionate way is probably the most effective and simple signal. When a man displays physical affection, it is clearly a sign that he is out of his cave.

Another way a man can assure a woman that he is out of the cave is by initiating conversation. Even if he doesn't have much to say, he can do this by asking her questions about her day. Although general questions like "How was your day?" are good, it is even better to then become more specific, like "How was your meeting with _____?" Although he may not care if she wants to learn about his day, his concern about her day makes her feel he is interested in her.

> **Showing interest is one of the most important secrets to opening a woman's heart.**

Initiating a conversation is particularly helpful because women today are often so much in their male sides that they don't even know they need to talk until they are asked. If she has been burned in the past while sharing her feelings, she will not consciously feel the need to talk.

FEBRUARY 10

How Men React to the Wave

*W*hen a man loves a woman, she begins to shine with love and fulfillment. Most men naively expect that shine to last forever. To expect her loving nature to be constant is like expecting the weather never to change and the sun to shine all the time. Life is filled with rhythms—day and night, hot and cold, summer and winter, spring and fall, cloudy and clear. Likewise, in a relationship, men and women have their own rhythms and cycles. Men pull back and then get close, while women rise and fall in their ability to love themselves and others.

> *Just as men pull back and then get close, women rise and fall in their ability to love themselves and others.*

A man mistakenly assumes that a woman's sudden change of mood is based solely on his behavior. When she is happy he takes credit, and when she is unhappy he also feels responsible. He may feel extremely frustrated because he doesn't know how to make things better. One minute she seems happy, and so he believes he is doing a good job. Then the next minute she is unhappy, and he is shocked because he thought he was doing so well. It is as though someone has come in and changed the score. In the first quarter he was winning, and suddenly he is losing.

By understanding the nature of a wave, he can be more supportive and less defensive when her wave crashes. The last thing a woman needs when she is on her way down is someone telling her why she shouldn't be down. What she needs is someone to be with her as she goes down, listen to her while she shares her feelings, and empathize with what she is going through.

Even if a man can't fully understand why a woman feels overwhelmed, he can offer his love, attention, and support. Just as women must learn to tolerate and eventually support a man's need to pull away, men must learn to tolerate and support a woman's ups and downs.

Why Women Need More Talk

*W*hen women don't feel free to talk during the course of a relationship, they disconnect from the natural happiness that comes when their female side is nurtured. Even more distressing, they may also lose the awareness of what they need as they lose touch with their female side. All they know is that something is missing, and generally the man in their lives gets blamed.

The more a woman disconnects from her female side, the less receptive she is to a man's support. Meanwhile, her partner feels frustrated because he can't fulfill her and feels powerless to change things. Some women don't even recognize that they need to talk. They mistakenly assume that they don't have time to talk or that talking will only make matters worse.

Talking can make matters worse if you don't have a good listener. When a woman has been deprived of good communication, she becomes more resistant to initiating conversation. Certainly it is her responsibility to recognize and fulfill this need, but just as certainly, a compassionate and understanding partner can help her.

To cope with the added stress of leaving the home to work, today's woman has a much greater need for partnership support. When she gets home, she needs to talk more. She needs the security of being able to open up and share feelings that may not always make sense or be related to the bottom line. She needs to feel that someone understands what she's going through and cares about her. Even if she seems somewhat resistant to talking, a wise man gently persists in drawing her out with caring questions.

FEBRUARY 12

Why Marriage?

*M*arriage is no longer just a commitment to ensure the security of a family. At a time when we are much more autonomous, the growth of love has become more important. People come together in love. There is no more powerful way to nurture that growth than to make a marriage commitment.

Marriage is the acknowledgment that our partner is special to us on all levels and that we are committed to the growth of love in the relationship. Marriage is a promise that we will hold our partner as more special than anyone else for our lifetime. This sacred commitment draws out the best in a man and gives a woman what she needs to grow in trust and openness. Her commitment helps her remember the feelings that brought them together at times when she has forgotten them.

A woman needs to feel special and cherished if she is to open up and grow in love and interdependence.

Without this commitment, something very important will be missing. For a woman to give a man the kind of special love, appreciation, acceptance, and trust that he wants, she must feel confident that her needs will also be met. She needs to feel that he adores, cares for, understands, and respects her so much that he will always be there for her. By settling for anything less, they will have less. The love they feel in their hearts will not have a chance to develop fully and be expressed.

FEBRUARY 13

What Romance Says

*W*hen a man does little things that say "I care, I understand what you feel, I know what you like, I am happy to do things for you, and you are not alone," he is directly fulfilling a woman's need for romance. When a man does little things without a woman having to ask, she feels deeply loved. If he forgets to do them, though, a wise woman graciously persists in reminding him by asking for them in a nondemanding manner.

***Romance for women is when
a man does things without her having to ask.***

A man receives love differently from a woman. He feels loved when she lets him know again and again that he is doing a good job of fulfilling her. Her good mood makes him feel loved. Even when she enjoys the weather, a part of him takes the credit. A man is happiest when a woman is fulfilled.

While a woman feels romanced by flowers, chocolates, and planned dates, a man's sense of romance is fueled by a woman's appreciation of him. When he does little things for her and she appreciates it a lot, he feels most romantic.

Romance for men is when a woman appreciates the things he does.

Women generally do not realize that what a man needs most is her loving message that he has fulfilled her. When she is happy about the things he provides for her, he feels loved. When he can do something for her, he lets in her love. The most important skill for loving a man is to catch him when he is doing something right and notice and appreciate him for it. The most significant mistake is taking him for granted.

A man feels loved when he gets the message that he has made a difference, that he has been helpful in some way, and that his partner benefits from his presence. The other way to love a man is to minimize his mistakes whenever possible with statements like "It's no big deal" or "It's okay." Downplaying disappointments makes him much more open to future requests and needs.

When a man does things for a woman and she is fulfilled, they both win.

~~~

The Importance of Commitment

*H*aving prepared ourselves in the earlier stages of dating, we gain the ability to know if we want to marry our dating partner. At some point we recognize our partner as our soul mate. Not only are we in love, we love this person so much that we want to spend the rest of our lives with them.

This recognition is only a glimpse. Although we are certain that our partner is right for us, this knowledge can later be doubted or forgotten. To make sure it is lasting, we must acknowledge and commit ourselves to it. It is important to strike while the iron is hot; otherwise, when it cools down, we may miss the opportunity.

By making the commitment to get married, we automatically strengthen and support this recognition. By acting on this feeling and becoming engaged, we make this delicate realization more solid, real, and grounded. It must be carefully nurtured and protected, like a little sprout shooting forth in spring.

> ***With the support of a heartfelt commitment,***
> ***love has a chance to grow stronger.***

Most men don't realize how important the proposal is to a woman. On Venus, the proposal is the second most cherished memory of a lifetime, after the wedding ceremony. Some men rebel against this idea because they don't realize how important it really is. Besides being one of the most important gifts a man can ever give, a great proposal paves the way for a great marriage.

At difficult times in the future, it will be helpful for the couple to look back to that very special moment and remember how they felt when their hearts were innocent, without any baggage, and they sincerely pledged their love to each other.

It is a wonderful gift for a man to create a memorable occasion. It will happen only once, so it's a good idea a put some extra thought into it. For the rest of her life a woman will tell the story of how her partner proposed.

FEBRUARY 15

Women and Romance; Men and Sex

A man often misunderstands a woman's real need for romance and may feel instead that she is withholding sex. When he wants sex and she is not readily in the mood, he easily misunderstands and feels rejected. He does not instinctively realize that a woman generally needs to feel loved and romanced before she can feel her hunger for sex.

Just as a woman needs good communication with her partner to feel loved and loving, a man needs sex. Certainly a man can feel loved in other ways, but the most powerful way a woman's love can touch his soul and open his heart is through great sex. While intimate conversation connects a woman to her heart, sex or the anticipation of sex connects a man to his heart.

※

The Art of Listening

*A*s a man learns to listen and interpret a woman's feelings correctly, communication becomes easier. As with any art, listening requires practice. Depending upon how adept a man is, sometimes he will just not be up to it. Until he is really good at it, there will be times when he can't do it without getting bent out of shape. A woman must remember that this is not a sign that he doesn't love her but a symptom of his inability to speak Venusian.

Sometimes a man doesn't realize that he is not up for listening until after a woman begins talking. If he becomes frustrated while listening, he should not try to continue—he'll just become increasingly upset. That does not serve him or her. Instead, the respectful thing to say is "I really want to hear what you are saying, but right now it is very difficult for me to listen. I think I need some time to think about what you have just said and then we can talk."

When misunderstandings arise, remember that we speak different languages; take the time necessary to translate what your partner really means or wants to say. This definitely takes practice, but it is well worth it.

Marriage vs. Friendship

*T*he one major characteristic that makes a marriage more than just a loving friendship is sex. Sex directly nurtures our male and female sides more than any other activity a couple can share. Great sex is soothing to a woman and helps keep her in touch with her feminine side, while it strengthens a man and keeps him in touch with his masculine side.

> **Sex has a tremendous power
> to bring us closer or push us apart.**

To create great sex, it is not enough for men or women to follow their ancient instincts. As times have changed, the quality of sex has become much more important. Our mothers couldn't tell us and our fathers didn't know the secrets of great sex. The ability to create lasting and passionate sex is not common knowledge, and it is not automatic.

Loving our partners is not enough. Just as the skills for relating and communicating have changed, so also have the skills for sex. To fulfill our partners in bed, new skills are required. We must remember not to take sex for granted. To keep sex great, both partners have to stay creative and considerate.

~∞~

What a Man Can Do When It's Difficult to Listen

*W*hen a man needs to pull away and a woman needs to talk, his trying to listen only makes matters worse. After a short time, he will either be judging her and possibly explode with anger or he will become incredibly tired or distracted, and she will become more upset. When he is not capable of listening attentively with caring, understanding, and respect, these three actions can help:

1. *Accept your limitations.*
   The first thing you need to do is accept that you need to pull away and have nothing to give. No matter how loving you want to be, you cannot listen attentively. Don't try to listen when you can't.

2. *Understand her pain.*
   Next you need to understand that she needs more than you can give at this moment. Her pain is valid. Don't make her wrong for needing more or for being hurt. It hurts to be abandoned when she needs your love. You are not wrong for needing space, and she is not wrong for wanting to be close. You may be afraid that she will not forgive you or trust you. She can be more trusting and forgiving if you are caring and understanding of her hurt.

3. *Avoid arguing and give reassurance.*
   By understanding her hurt, you won't make her wrong for being upset and in pain. Although you can't give the support she wants

and needs, you can avoid making it worse by arguing. Reassure her that you will be back and that then you will be able to give her the support she deserves.

Two Kinds of Men; One Kind of Behavior

*T*here are two kinds of men. One will become incredibly defensive and stubborn when a woman tries to change him; the other will agree to change but later will forget and revert back to the old behavior. A man resists either actively or passively.

When a man does not feel loved just the way he is, he will either consciously or unconsciously repeat the behavior that is not being accepted. He feels an inner compulsion to repeat the behavior until he feels loved and accepted.

> *A man is free to be the best he can be*
> *when he feels accepted just the way he is.*

For a man to improve himself, he needs to feel loved in an accepting way. Otherwise he defends himself and stays the same. He needs to feel accepted just the way he is, and then he, on his own, will look for ways to improve. When a woman lets go of feeling responsible to change a man, he is free to feel more responsible to change himself.

~~~~

Passionate Monogamy

*F*or some people, the thought of having sex with one person all their life seems too boring. They want more excitement. When you learn how to make sex spontaneous and not mechanical, it doesn't have to become boring. Over time, the feeling of sex can continue to change and passion can continue to grow.

> **When you change the way you are having sex,**
> **then you don't need to change partners.**

The secret of success in marriage is good communication and great sex. For most women to continue feeling sexually responsive, monogamy is essential. Many men don't realize why monogamy is so important. They don't instinctively understand that monogamy ensures that a woman continues to feel special and loved. If she is not feeling loved in this way, she cannot continue to open herself to him. Trust is essential for a woman to continue getting turned on.

Men also have special needs if they are to experience passionate monogamy. It is easy for a man to be turned on in the beginning, but it is not so automatic to keep that attraction. It is not enough for a man to love a woman; he needs to feel that she is attracted to him, she is open to him, and she is an equal partner in creating a great sex life. Instead of feeling he has to somehow convince her to have sex, he needs to feel that he has an eager and willing partner. Her warmth, openness, and enthusiasm around sex go a long way to support his continued desire.

FEBRUARY 21

Reacting to Stress

*P*roblems between men and women arise when one sex expects the other sex to think, feel, and behave the way they do. Women frequently misinterpret a man's love by evaluating his behavior according to feminine standards, and vice versa. Love is expressed differently on Mars and Venus.

This mutual misunderstanding arises because men and women react differently under stress. Men tend to prioritize and focus on what is most urgent, while women tend to expand and become more acutely aware of the variety of problems and demands being placed upon them.

> **Under stress, men tend to overfocus**
> **while women tend to overexpand.**

The drawback of overfocusing is that a man will tend to forget other responsibilities and attach little importance to them. The drawback of overexpanding is that a woman becomes overwhelmed with everything that needs to be done and may have difficulty deciding what needs to be done first.

Ideally, a relationship should nurture and assist us in coping with stress. Without an understanding of our different stress reactions, we tend to misinterpret each other and make things worse. It is hard for a woman to understand a man's overfocusing: to become oblivious to the needs of someone she cares about while solving a problem at work is not one of her common experiences. On the other hand, it is hard for a man to understand why his partner may become so overwhelmed by the problems of her day.

Given this common difference, it is easy to see how we misinterpret each other and then react to our partner with criticism or judgment. It is hard to respond in a caring, understanding, and respectful way when you assume that your partner *should* think and feel the way you do. No matter how committed we are to improving our relationships, it is impossible to make significant advances without reevaluating our hidden assumptions.

We mistakenly assume that our partner
should think and feel the way we do.

The vast majority of conflicts between men and women stem from one basic misunderstanding: we assume that we are the same, when in many ways men and women are as different as if they really were from different planets. Without an understanding of how we are different, all our efforts to unravel the mysteries of keeping love's magic alive cannot begin to bear fruit.

~~~~~

Making Little Changes

*T*o enrich our relationships, making little changes is often much more effective than trying to make big changes. When a seed grows in the garden, it is always through a series of little changes. Big changes generally require some suppression of who we truly are, and this defeats the purpose of making a change. Ideally, relationships should nurture being more of who we are and not less.

For example, when a man goes to his cave, giving some reassurance that he will be back is a small change that a man can make without changing his nature. To make this change, he must realize that women really do need some reassurance, especially if they are to worry less. If a man doesn't understand the differences between men and women, then he cannot comprehend why his sudden silence is such a cause for worry. By giving some reassurance, he can remedy the situation.

> **When a man pulls away, giving a little reassurance**
> **that he will be back can make a big difference.**

When a man goes into his cave or becomes quiet, he is saying "I need some time to think about this. Please stop talking to me. I will be back." He doesn't realize that a woman may hear "I don't love you. I can't stand to listen to you. I am leaving, and I am never coming back!" To counteract this message and to give her the correct message, he can learn to say the four magic words: "I will be back."

It is amazing how the simple words "I will be back" or "Let's talk about this a little later" can make such a profound difference.

If a woman felt abandoned or rejected by her father or if her mother felt rejected by her husband, then she (the child) will be even more sensitive to feeling abandoned. For this reason, she should never be judged for needing this reassurance. Similarly, a man should not be judged for needing the cave.

FEBRUARY 23

Feelings Are Not Facts

*W*hen a man expresses a feeling, it is more like a fact—something he believes to be true but doesn't have a lot of objective evidence to back up. This is not what a woman means when she shares her feelings. For women, feelings are much less about the outer world and more about their *experience* of the outer world. For women, feelings and facts are very different animals.

For women, feelings are much less about the outer world and more about their experience of the outer world.

When a woman shares her feelings, a man needs constantly to remind himself that she does not mean that her feelings are facts. He need not argue or defend himself. If her feelings are negative, and she is allowed to share them without argument or interruption, she will gradually have more positive feelings. A wise man focuses on trying to be understanding and empathetic and holds back from trying to solve the problem.

FEBRUARY 24

Remembering Our Differences

*R*ight understanding between men and women starts with realizing that we are all individual and unique and that it is very easy to misunderstand each other. To grow in understanding and to succeed in our relationships, we need always to come back to remembering that we are different and that the differences are okay. By understanding and respecting our differences, we can truly build bridges that will unite us. At times of frustration, disappointment, and worry, it is helpful to remember that:

Appearances do not always reflect reality; men and women react differently under stress.

What may be easy for you to ask may be difficult for others to ask.

What may be easy for you to hear may be painful for others to hear.

What you think should be helpful to others may not be—even if it is helpful to you.

People express their love in different ways.

~~~

When a Man Doesn't Need Help

A man may start to feel smothered when a woman tries to comfort him or to help him solve a problem. To him unsolicited help feels as though she doesn't trust him to handle his problems. Her assistance may make him feel controlled, as if she is treating him like a child, or he may feel she wants to change him.

This doesn't mean that a man does not need comforting love. Women need to understand that they are nurturing a man when they abstain from offering unsolicited advice to solve his problems. He needs her loving support, but in a different way than she thinks. To resist correcting a man or trying to improve him are ways to nurture him.

> **Giving advice can be nurturing**
> **only if a man directly asks for it.**

A man looks for advice or help only after he has done what he can do alone. If he receives too much assistance or receives it too soon, he will lose his sense of power and strength. He becomes either lazy or insecure. Instinctively men support one another by not offering advice or help unless specifically approached and asked. In coping with problems, a man knows he has first to go a certain distance by himself. Then, if he needs help, he can ask for it without losing his strength, power, and dignity.

Wearing Different Glasses

Men and women see the world as if each sex were wearing different glasses. In a generalized way, men see the world from a focused perspective, while women see the world from a more expanded perspective. Both perceptions are equally accurate.

Masculine awareness tends to relate one thing to another in a sequential way, gradually building a complete picture. It is a perspective that relates one part to another part in terms of producing a whole.

Feminine awareness intuitively takes in the whole picture, gradually discovers the parts within, then explores how the parts are all related to the whole. This approach places more emphasis on context than on content.

Although we see the world differently, one way is not better than the other.

This difference in orientation greatly affects values, priorities, instincts, and interest. Since feminine open awareness perceives how we are interrelated, women naturally take a greater interest in love, relationships, communication, sharing, cooperation, intuition, and harmony. Since masculine-focused awareness perceives how parts make up a whole, men have a greater interest in producing results, achieving goals, power, competition, work, logic, and efficiency. By respecting and appreciating our differences, we gain the benefit of our partner's approach and perspective.

꙳

Overgiving Is Not Dysfunctional

*M*any popular books leave the impression that giving too much is dysfunctional. Although giving too much is a problem, we must also remember that it is a blessing to have a giving and generous nature. To feel love, we must continue to give of ourselves. Women who give too much are just following their healthy feminine instincts to give freely of themselves.

A woman's natural inclination to give unconditionally becomes problematic only when her business and personal relationships do not nurture her in return. Giving too much becomes a problem only when a woman is not adept at getting back the nurturing support she needs to continue giving.

> ***The solution to giving too much
> is to practice receiving more in return.***

To compensate for overgiving, a woman needs to practice asking for support, a skill most women were not taught while growing up. Unfortunately, most girls are taught how to please others rather than how to be pleased. To find balance, women who give too much need to practice giving more to themselves as well. The most important gift you can give yourself is time—time to do whatever you want.

She Needs Validation, and He Needs Approval

*W*hen a man does not object to or argue with a woman's feelings and wants but instead understands and confirms their validity, a woman feels truly loved. A man's validating attitude confirms a woman's right to feel the way she does. It is important to remember that one can validate her point of view while having a different point of view. When a man learns how to let a woman know that he has this validating attitude, he is assured of getting the approval that he primarily needs.

> ***As a woman is nurtured by a man's validation,***
> ***a man is nurtured by her approval.***

Deep inside, every man wants to be his woman's hero or knight in shining armor. The sign that he has passed her tests is her approval. A woman's approving attitude acknowledges the goodness in a man and expresses overall satisfaction with him. Remember, giving approval to a man doesn't always mean agreeing with him. An approving attitude recognizes or looks for the good reasons behind what he does. When he receives the approval he needs, it becomes easier for him to validate her feelings.

❧ MARCH ❧

Imagine, Experience, Protect

*M*arch is a time of rebirth, when old can suddenly turn new. Out of winter's bleakness emerges a higher sense of life, and we begin again to imagine all its opportunities. Nature's wonders bloom around us where just days before they went unfound.

These fragile and emerging blossoms are a metaphor for our relationships: women experience the need to love and be loved, while men experience the need to provide and protect. As she looks to him for love and connection, he looks to her for meaning and purpose.

Spring comes and arouses our senses and stirs our imaginations. For many men it comes as a surprise to experience once again the rising waves of love that accompany the pleasure of physical intimacy. For some women it can be a surprise to feel once again the rising waves of excitement and anticipation as the beauty and romance of spring are awakened.

These revelations allow us to appreciate the essence of a lasting and loving relationship. Passion can grow in time. Just as nature moves through the icy winter to be reborn in spring, so also can our deepest feelings of love, hope, and joy be renewed and reborn. Just when we begin to believe that the best is behind us, we are surprised by new glimpses of an even greater fulfillment.

The Four Doorways to Intimacy

*T*here are four doorways to connecting and experiencing true intimacy—physical, emotional, mental, and spiritual. Unless we nurture each of these different aspects of who we are, we are not ready to become deeply intimate in a relationship. If we rush into being too intimate on one level before we are connected at other levels, the results may be counterproductive.

When couples have physical intimacy before being connected on the other levels as well, the man generally ends up pulling away while the woman feels more needy. Some neediness and some pulling away are fine, but when we are not prepared on all levels, these two reactions are even stronger.

> **Sex is best when we have also connected emotionally, mentally, and spiritually.**

When we are not connected at the higher levels, after sex a man may pull away so intensely that he doesn't come back to the relationship. A woman will feel so needy that she will begin to pursue the man as he pulls away and turn him off. By first opening all four doorways, a man and a woman become ready to experience true intimacy.

Physical connection is through sex, emotional connection is through affection, mental connection is through showing interest, and spiritual connection is through unconditional love. Whether we are dating or married for many years, each of the four aspects of our being must be enlivened for intimacy to grow. To sustain intimacy on any one level, we must make sure we nurture our connection at each of the four levels: physical, emotional, mental, and spiritual.

MARCH 2

The Golden Twenty Minutes

*B*y allotting an extra twenty minutes three or four days a week, a man can do wonders to nurture a woman's female side. Not only will she be happier, but he will begin to get the appreciation and acceptance he needs when he gets home. No matter how overworked or exhausted she feels, he can, with a small amount of concentrated attention, focus his love and caring in ways that make a big difference.

These twenty minutes of attention and support become golden when he devotes the first twenty minutes on his arrival home to her exclusively. For twenty minutes, she is his number one priority. For twenty minutes, he must give his attention to her as if he were assisting his boss or his most important client. During that time, by showing interest and helping out, he can have a tremendous impact on her life.

> **For twenty minutes, he should give her his attention as if he were assisting his boss or his most important client.**

If she is exhausted or in a bad mood, instead of leaving her alone he should persist in being present. In conversation he should try to understand what her feelings are and what her day was like. By responding with sympathy and not solutions or suggestions, he can have a tremendously nurturing effect.

By addressing and nurturing the female side of her being, a man can respond compassionately and skillfully to a woman feeling exhausted and overwhelmed. By making her feel special, he can awaken the romantic feelings that make her so attractive to him. By clearly delineating her male and female aspects, he can effectively work at steering her toward feeling like herself again.

MARCH 3

The Unfolding Process of Sharing

*S*ometimes, when a woman needs to share, she doesn't know exactly what she wants to say. She may have so much to share, she doesn't know where to start. Or she may need time to share a progression of feelings and thoughts before she discovers the point she wants to make. A man also goes through this preparation process but in a different way. He ponders things within, comes to a conclusion, then shares it outwardly.

A woman, on the other hand, just wants to share and connect. She wants to enjoy being together. For her, communication is not just a sharing of information, it is a sharing of herself. It is a basis for intimacy. It is fulfilling and centering.

> *For a woman, communication is not just a sharing of information, it is a sharing of herself.*

For a woman, sharing is a gradual unfolding, and she may need to be drawn out. She may not know exactly what she wants to say, but (1) she wants to connect and feel in a relationship, and (2) communication is her major means of connecting and relating.

When an upset woman shares her feelings, it is as though she is sharing the contents of her purse. She needs time to clean out that purse without being judged for having so much in it or for not knowing exactly what she does have. If she begins to expand outward, a man can imagine that she is just taking everything out of her purse. When it is all out, she will feel much lighter, and he will have served a very important role.

When a woman is sharing what's inside her, if she has a respectful, attentive, and caring listener, she will feel safe to empty out her purse (her inner feelings). Once everything is out, she will feel much more centered and loving. She will greatly appreciate the support.

MARCH 4

Why Romance Works

When a man plans a date, handles the tickets, drives the car, and takes care of all the small details, that is romance. When a man is responsible for taking care of things, a woman can relax and enjoy feeling taken care of. It is like a mini vacation that helps her come back to her female side.

> **For a woman, romance is like a mini vacation**
> **that helps her come back to her female side.**

Romantic moments are particularly helpful for women who don't feel comfortable sharing their feelings. On a romantic date, without having to talk about her feelings a woman can feel acknowledged, adored, understood, and supported. She receives the benefits of talking without having to talk.

A man's romantic behavior shows repeatedly that he acknowledges her. By anticipating her needs, he signals that he understands and respects her. These kinds of actions give her the same support that talking does. In both cases, she feels heard.

~~~~~

What a Man Can Do for a Woman

*T*o support a woman, a man must understand that deep inside she longs to relax, let go, and surrender to someone she trusts to support and care for her. This is the true inner need of the female side. When this side of her is nurtured, she can feel and express the loving side of her nature.

Often, because she judges her need for help as unacceptable or too strong, she unconsciously replaces it with a false need. The replacement need emerges as an urgent calling to fulfill the needs of others. She feels as if her happiness is based on providing fulfillment for others instead of getting her own needs satisfied. In a sense, she becomes the responsible and caring man she wishes could fulfill her.

> ***A woman may deny her need for help and compensate by becoming more giving to others.***

This insight is valuable for both women and men. When a woman is becoming overly responsible, instead of criticizing her for doing too much, a man can realize that she needs help in getting back to her feminine side. Traditional romantic rituals in which the man takes care of the woman help her to be as comfortable with receiving as she is with giving.

~~~~

Our Dark Sides

*W*hen a man is unable to support himself or get the support he needs in stressful situations, inevitably his dark side will be provoked. When he feels hurt, offended, or wounded, he becomes withdrawn, mean, and uncaring. Similarly, when a woman doesn't get the support she needs, her dark side emerges. When she loses her centredness, she becomes rigid, opinionated, and mistrusting.

> *While men can become mean and uncaring, women can become opinionated and mistrusting.*

By recognizing our dark sides, we can then take responsibility for changing our dark attitudes. At such times, we should minimize expecting our partner to change before we change. When our dark side emerges, it is up to us to release it. This is best accomplished by nurturing our relationship with ourselves, friends, family, and God or a higher power. As we feel more loved, we can then be more loving to our partners.

The Art of Listening to a Woman

A woman can most successfully cope with the stress of experiencing nonnurturing relationships in the goal-oriented work world by coming home and experiencing a loving, caring, and cooperative relationship. The most important element of a nurturing relationship that is generally missing at work is nongoal-oriented conversation. By talking or sharing without having to get to the bottom line, without having to solve the problem, a woman is gradually released from the domination of her masculine side.

> *By sharing in a nongoal-oriented way at home,*
> *a woman can nurture the feminine part of her*
> *that is not nurtured at work.*

Talking in a nonlinear, unedited, emotional way is especially beneficial when her listener understands that by merely articulating her problems, she can put them aside. She does not have to solve them to feel better.

That a woman can forget the problems of her day by remembering them is a concept foreign to most men, who generally banish the problems of the day by not talking about them. To recall the problems of the day will often just make a man feel worse. When he does bring up problems, he is generally looking for solutions. Most men don't instinctively realize how valuable it is for a woman to discuss problems without focusing on finding solutions.

While it is important to men to not talk, it is equally important to women to talk. This apparent incompatibility is actually a perfect fit. It just requires a new job description. The art of listening to a woman does not entail solving problems or offering advice. A male listener's goal should be helping his partner regain her feminine/masculine balance by simply listening and not offering solutions.

This new job description clarifies his goal and directs him to watch and listen, giving her the sympathy she craves, not the solutions. To develop skill in listening, a man needs to recognize that when a woman is upset and seems to be demanding solutions to her problems, it is only because she is still operating primarily from her male side. By not responding with solutions, he assists her in finding her female side; she will then eventually feel better. Men are easily tricked into thinking that if they can give solutions, women will then feel better.

Remembering this is particularly helpful when a man feels that a woman is upset with him. To explain why she shouldn't be so upset with him only makes matters worse. Although he may have disappointed her in some way, he must remember that her real complaint is that she is not being heard or nurtured as a woman. When she feels heard, she is more capable of bestowing on him the appreciation and acknowledgment he has earned.

~~~~

Mind Reading

*F*aulty communication between the sexes is largely due to mistaken assumptions. One of the most common of those assumptions manifests itself as what we can call mind reading. Since men and women do not realize how different they are, they assume that they know what the other is thinking or feeling before it has been clearly stated.

True, women are quite accurate when mind reading other women because they are already so similar. Likewise, men can accurately read the minds of other men. When men and women start mind reading each other, trouble is inevitable.

> **Men and women mistakenly assume that they can correctly interpret or anticipate each other.**

For example, sometimes in a conversation a man prematurely decides that he knows what a woman is saying. His error lies in assuming that she started out making the point she wanted to make as a man would. He may be listening and then, before the speaker is finished, says, "I got it, I got it." This works fine with another man, but to a woman his statement is preposterous. She knows that he can't know what she intends to say, because many times even she doesn't know. While sharing, she is in the process of finding out what she feels, thinks, or wants.

A man needs to understand that if a woman needs to talk, and if his desire is to support her, then his purpose in listening is not just to get the gist of what she is saying but to help her get it out. As she gets it out without being interrupted, her view might change midstream or she might completely change the subject. She may ask questions and then start answering them.

By expecting this to happen, he can avoid feeling frustrated. He needs to remember that just as he has to mull over his problems before talking about them, a woman needs to talk about her problems before she will have a definite opinion. If she feels overwhelmed by difficulties, just by talking about them she may feel better.

MARCH 9

~~~

Why Romance Is Important

Romance is so important today because it helps a woman to come back to her female side. For most of the day she is doing a traditionally male job that requires her to move more to her male side. To find relief, she needs her partner's help to return to her female side.

Romance brings a woman back to her female side.

Romance clearly places the woman in the feminine role of being special and cared for. When a man passionately focuses on fulfilling her needs, she is able to release her tendency to take care of others. For romance to stay alive, there must be good communication, particularly for her, and great sex, particularly for him.

✧✦✧

Why Women Become Overwhelmed

*W*hen a woman is upset, she needs time to explore her feelings by sharing before she is able to be her loving, appreciative, accepting, and trusting self. When she is unable to explore her feelings, she becomes overwhelmed, overreacts, and then feels exhausted. At that point she requires even more time to come back to her center. To lighten her load, what she needs most from a man is his caring and attention, respect for her needs, and understanding.

When a woman has no one to share with, she begins to feel the weight of all her responsibilities.

A man typically goes into judgment and blame when a woman is upset or overwhelmed. She needs instead for him to listen and support her without trying to fix her or correct her. He must consciously resist trying to give advice or telling her how she should feel; otherwise she will feel invalidated. When men truly realize how they unknowingly hurt women in this way, they automatically become more considerate and respectful.

❧❧❧

What Makes Sex Better

*F*or many men, it comes as a surprise to experience that mental and emotional intimacy can be as fulfilling as physical intimacy. When a man eventually tastes the fulfillment of complete physical intimacy with someone with whom he also shares emotional, mental, and spiritual intimacy, he cannot go back.

> ***After years of growing together in love,***
> ***sex becomes richer and more fulfilling.***

Even after being married for many years, it is important to reflect sometimes on how satisfying it is to make love with someone you really know and love with all your heart. To love someone after seeing both the worst and the best of them is to experience real love.

Just to have sex when he could make love is like eating junk food when he could have a Thanksgiving feast. Why settle for less? It may take more time and energy, but it is real and lasting. Yet it is still important to have all kinds of sex—sex after a romantic evening or simply quickie sex in between appointments. When a man feels that his partner is as enthusiastic about sex as he is, then he is free to open his heart more fully.

MARCH 12

Stress and the Emotionally Absent Man

*T*he more stress a man has at work, the more detached he may be at home. When spoken to, he may pick up a magazine and begin to read it. This is not a conscious insult, nor does it mean that he is not interested in you. He is unconsciously picking up the magazine to distract himself from listening to you because most of his mind is still focused on the problems of work. Ultimately, by reading a magazine or watching TV, he is attempting to forget the stress of his day.

A man under stress needs to take some time to forget what is bothering him before he can focus on his family.

Instead of taking this personally, a woman can remember that he is from Mars. Instead of being insulted, politely ask for his full attention. If he gets distracted again, pause until he notices that you are waiting for his complete attention. Remember, his lack of attentiveness is not a reflection of his love but a symptom of stress. For the woman, persistence is necessary.

When a woman attempts to engage in conversation, I suggest that men get in the habit of putting down the newspaper or magazine—not just in their lap but completely out of their hands—when listening. If there is a TV on, it is best to turn it off until the exchange is complete. These little physical actions increase your ability to turn off work and shift your focus to the family or relationship.

Ultimately, what will free a man from the stresses of work is sex. Sexual release, even if just a quickie or alone in the shower, will assist him in temporarily letting go of his worries and then connecting with his partner. While a woman needs romantic attention to fully enjoy sex, a man may need a quickie to forget his problems and reconnect to his partner and her needs. If a woman is consistent in satisfying a man's sexual needs, it is important that she ask for and get the romantic attention she requires at other times.

MARCH 13

The Fifteen-Minute Delay

*S*ometimes when we are upset, we don't realize until later what we have said. Often, if a woman is upset and shares her feelings, it may take fifteen minutes to reflect on what she has said. After such consideration, she begins to appreciate a man's strong support. She thinks, "I really unloaded on him and he wasn't mean to me. He really tried to be considerate. He is wonderful. Let me think what can I do for him."

Sometimes there is a fifteen-minute delay before a woman can really appreciate that a man is there for her.

If a man says something in frustration, like "What's the point" or "This was sure a waste of time" or "If this doesn't help, why do we even bother," it can undo all the good he did. It will be as though he gave a gift and then took it back. And to a woman, that is worse than not giving it in the first place.

That fifteen minutes when she is reflecting on what she has said is a very vulnerable time for a woman. If a man is trying to tell her that she is wrong, or if she feels she has to defend herself, then it is very hard for her to see her mistakes and release any negative feelings she is holding onto.

MARCH 14

A Man's Confidence

A woman can sense when a man is confident, and she automatically begins to relax and feel assured that she will get what she needs. When a man does not feel confident, a woman begins to worry. Her feminine side, which wants to relax and receive, panics, and her masculine side rises up to protect her and make sure she gets what she needs.

> *Confidence in a man makes a woman breathe deeper, relax,*
> *and open up to receive the support he has to offer.*

Confidence does not mean that a man has to be perfect, nor does he have to have all the answers. Confidence is a can-do attitude. He knows that no matter what happens, there is always a solution. Even if he doesn't have the answer, he is confident that he can, and will, find one. A confident attitude reassures a woman that everything will be all right.

MARCH 15

Forming Opinions

*M*uch conflict can be avoided by understanding how differently men and women form and express opinions. In general, women take longer to form opinions and make decisions. They take additional time and care to consider various points of view and to gather all available information. In the process of forming an opinion, they tend to be open to other points of view and are careful to let others know that they do not claim to be absolutely right. Once they have formed an opinion or made a decision, they tend to become very fixed and definite.

Men form and express opinions in the opposite way. A man quickly forms an opinion or conclusion based on what he already knows. Then he tests it out by proclaiming it as if he were certain. By experiencing various reactions to his opinion, he then reassesses its accuracy. If others agree with his opinion, he feels more definite. If others have differing opinions, he may weigh their merits against his own and then change his view.

> *In forming opinions, women appear to be*
> *more inclusive of other points of view.*

A woman misinterprets a man's conviction by assuming that he has made up his mind without including her. His definite style is easily misunderstood as an unwillingness to hear her point of view. Instead of appreciating his openness to her point of view, she feels hurt, excluded, and defensive.

By understanding our differing styles, we can respect and integrate them both. In forming opinions and then making decisions, truly balanced men and women understand the creative value of openly sharing thoughts and feelings, yet they also respect the value of self-reflection and thinking a problem over before seeking input from others. Being open to and respectful of our partner's style of reasoning will help to avoid conflict.

꧁꧂

Emotional Self-Defense

*T*he instincts that sent warriors boldly into battle to defend themselves and protect their loved ones come into play when a modern man tries to listen to a modern woman. To prevail, he must learn to duck and dodge.

Ducking and dodging require new mental strategies for correctly interpreting the situation. Instead of reacting to blame and criticism, a man learns to hear the loving message in her words and responds in ways that diminish friction and conflict. Ducking and dodging allow a man to keep his cool and respond respectfully to a woman's need to communicate.

When he listens to a woman without ducking and dodging, he will be repeatedly assaulted by her words and begin to feel blamed, criticized, unacknowledged, misunderstood, rejected, mistrusted, or unappreciated. No matter how much he loves her, after about three direct hits, he will no longer be capable of listening to her in a supportive way. War breaks out.

> ***When a man doesn't duck or dodge what appears to be an attack, he loses his ability to respond in a supportive manner.***

When a man is struck by a woman's words, it is much harder for him to restrain his ancient warrior instincts to intimidate, threaten, or retaliate. Once these defensive responses are triggered, he will attempt either to change her mind by arguing or to protect her from his own aggressive reactions by withdrawing emotionally.

To dodge criticism successfully, a man needs to remember that all feelings are temporary. By listening to a woman's negative emotions, he allows her the opportunity to discover her positive feelings as well. In return, a woman can help him duck and dodge by making supportive comments.

While men are learning to duck and dodge, women can learn to pause and prepare. Before or even while sharing feelings that may sound as if she is blaming or attacking, she can pause and prepare him by saying something like "I know this may sound like blame. I want you to know that it's not all your fault, and I really appreciate that you are listening to my feelings."

If she notices that he has become upset, she could pause and say, "It makes sense to me that you feel frustrated with all these feelings. Although it may not look like it, it really is helpful for me to get this out." These words are validating to him and will help him cool off.

MARCH 17

Male Tunnel Vision

*F*ocused awareness can make men incredibly determined and efficient, but it can also make them oblivious to another's needs and to priorities not directly related to their primary goal. Consequently, when a man is focused on a particular task or problem, he may not notice the signs of growing distress in his environment, family, relationship, or even within his own body.

When he is overly focused, temporarily he does not feel pain or hurt, nor does he acknowledge this in others. He unconsciously negates the importance of needs that are not directly related to his focus. If his wife and children are hurting or upset, his reaction is that they shouldn't hurt and they shouldn't be upset. This kind of invalidation and denial is very hurtful to others and destructive to relationships.

> **When tunnel vision sets in, a man easily forgets**
> **why he is working so hard in the first place.**

When a man is under a lot of stress and this tunnel vision sets in, the solution is not to find another job in which to bury himself or to mask the problem through drinking or drugs. The cure for tunnel vision is to create the emotional support he needs and to assess his real priorities and values. He needs to remember why he is working so hard in the first place.

By remembering the needs of his wife and family and then taking some time for them, he can come back to his work with greater creativity. Sometimes before he can give to his family, he needs to take some time for himself. Rather than focusing on solving the problems at work, he should be encouraged to do something he enjoys doing. Once he is reconnected to his feelings, he can be there more for his loved ones.

MARCH 18

Growing Together in Love

*F*inding the right person for you is like hitting the center of a target in archery. To aim and hit the center takes a lot of practice. Some people may hit the center right away, but most do not. In a similar way, most people date several people before finding the right one. Some people take much longer than necessary because something is missing in their approach. By exploring this metaphor from archery, we can clearly see what may be lacking.

Imagine that you aim for the target and you miss. Your shot is too far to the left. By simply acknowledging that you went too far to the left, your mind will automatically self-correct, and next time you will shoot more to the right. Through a series of attempts, your mind will continue to self-correct, and you will eventually hit the target.

It is the same in relationships. Each time you go out and discover that this is the wrong person for you, your mind will self-correct, and the next time you will feel more attracted to someone who is closer to being the right person. Correctly assessing someone is important for fine-tuning our ability to be attracted to someone who is either right for us or at least closer to the target. When a relationship ends, rather than feel as if we were burned or we wasted precious time, we can be grateful for the opportunity to move on to find real love.

Good endings always make for good beginnings.

By forgiving an ex-partner and ending a relationship with love, our chances of hitting the target next time go up. It is easier to forgive when we recognize that things didn't work out because our mate was not the right partner for us. Forgiveness keeps our hearts open. Likewise in a relationship, when we forgive our partner for mistakes, we are free to love again. When we are more loving, we give them the opportunity to love us back.

When we forgive a partner, we are adjusting our expectations to accept our partner even though they are not perfect. This unconditional love is a challenge, but it is what brings out the best in ourselves and our partner. By learning to forgive our partner and not to demand perfection, we are able to grow together in love.

※※

Active and Receptive Interest

*T*here are basically two kinds of interest: active and receptive. Active interest is what we feel when we have a goal in mind: it motivates action to achieve a goal, thrives on achievement, and comes from a place of desire and confidence. Active interest wants to serve, while receptive interest wants to be served. Receptive interest is what we feel when we are openly considering the value of what is being offered: it is motivated to create opportunities to receive, thrives in response to support, and comes from a place of preference and worthiness.

These two kinds of interest are reciprocal in their effect on each other. When a man is very actively interested in a woman, his active interest will usually generate feelings of receptive interest in her. If a woman is receptively interested in a man, it will generate his active interest in her.

> *A woman's receptive interest in a man*
> *inspires his active interest in her.*

This is why it is important for women not to give more than they are getting. When a man receives more than he is giving, he tends to become too receptive and loses touch with his active interest in pursuing and providing for the woman.

MARCH 20

A Woman's Responsibility

*E*ven though a woman is more aware of the needs in a relationship, that does not make her solely responsible for solving its problems. But she is responsible for getting her own needs fulfilled—in two main ways. First, she must communicate her needs and wishes without resenting her partner. Second, she must get her needs fulfilled from a variety of sources and not make her partner the source of her dissatisfaction or the sole source of her fulfillment.

MARCH 21

The Springtime of Love

*F*alling in love is like springtime. We feel as though we will be happy forever. We cannot imagine not loving our partner. It is a time of innocence. Love seems eternal. It is a magical time when everything seems perfect and works effortlessly. We dance together in harmony and rejoice in our good fortune.

In the springtime of love our partner seems to be the perfect fit.

After the springtime of love, we are faced with the sweat and toil of summertime. That is followed by the fruits of our labor in the harvest season. During the summer, it may seem as if we have lost the magic of love, but in the autumn we once again experience a more grounded love, a real love.

Feeling secure in our love, the autumn of love is followed by the winter of love. This is a time when it seems love is gone. But only temporarily. Rather than look to our partners to fill us up, we need to pull back into ourselves and fill up with love. This is a time to release any blame and take time to nurture our needs without depending on our partner.

As we fill up with love, we are once again amazed by the return of springtime. Once again, when our hearts are full and begin to overflow, we feel the bliss of falling in love. Cherish the memories of this perfect love to support you during the summer and winter seasons of love.

MARCH 22

How Women Can Deal with Tunnel Vision

*W*omen are naturally gifted with an intuitive awareness of the needs of others. But open awareness can be a mixed blessing when a woman's partner is experiencing tunnel vision. While the man thinks everything is fine in the relationship, the woman is burdened by her awareness of all the problems.

When he is not sharing this burden, she mistakenly assumes that he is happy with the relationship. When he acts as though everything is fine, while she sees problems, she gets the message that she is much too demanding or that he doesn't care and will never do anything to change.

> *When a man acts as though everything is fine,*
> *while she sees problems,*
> *it makes a woman feel even more burdened.*

This feminine awareness of a relationship's problems becomes a burden to her when he is not willing to hear and validate her awareness. When he denies the validity of her needs and perceptions, she then feels that the burden of the relationship and the family rests on her shoulders. She feels alone and unsupported. No wonder women become frustrated when men act as though everything is fine.

With this new understanding of tunnel vision, a woman can correctly conclude that her partner appears satisfied only because he is unconscious of the problems. She can realize that if he were aware of the problems, he too would be upset or would be motivated to improve things.

Both partners are equally responsible for creating a good relationship, but their roles are different. The woman will naturally be more aware of the relationship's needs and problems.

꼭꼭

Learning from Our Mistakes

*S*ometimes, as we get older, we just assume that things will be the same. We don't realize that patterns can and do change. While dating, men and women hold back from getting involved when they assume that every relationship has to be the same. It doesn't. When we take time to learn from the mistakes in our past relationships, we can have confidence that our future relationships will be better.

> **When we learn from our mistakes, we hold the power to improve our relationships.**

In a long-term relationship, we get caught up in thinking that our partner cannot change. This limited belief will not only prevent them from growing but prevent us as well. When we make our well-being dependent on our partner's changes, we hold both of us back. The best and only way to create change in a relationship is to focus on changing ourselves.

It takes two to create a relationship. When one person makes changes, it definitely changes the relationship. Change is possible, but only if we focus on changing ourselves. Trying to improve a relationship by trying to change our partner never works.

Women Are Still from Venus

*A*lthough modern women are independent and assertive, their female natures still seek out strong men who provide and protect. They still want a provider and protector but in a different sense.

Women now look to men to provide the emotional climate in which they can safely explore and express their feelings. When a man can listen to a woman's feelings and allow her to articulate them without responding negatively, she is not only very appreciative but more attracted to him as a result.

> **Providing emotional support requires
> a new strength and skill from men.**

By ducking and dodging, a man can avoid getting upset and will create a new dimension of protection for the woman he loves. This new ability and strength not only helps her but ensures that he too will get the love he deserves and wants.

Security is the most important gift a contemporary man can give a woman. In hunter/nurturer societies, that security was primarily physical. Today, it is emotional as well. A woman seeks to feel safe to be herself, to share herself without fear of rejection, invalidation, or retribution of some kind. Learning to provide this security is a gradual process. As a woman grows in trust she can open up to a man with greater love and acceptance of him.

What Makes Women Happy

*W*omen are happy when they believe their needs will be met. When a woman is upset, overwhelmed, confused, exhausted, or hopeless, what she needs most is simple companionship. She needs to feel she is not alone. She needs to feel loved and cherished.

Empathy, understanding, validation, and compassion go a long way to assist her in becoming more receptive and appreciative of his support. Men don't realize this, because their Martian instincts tell them it's best to be alone when they are upset.

**Under stress a woman needs intimacy
while often a man needs space.**

When a woman is upset, out of respect a man will leave her alone, or if he stays, he makes matters worse by trying to solve her problems. He does not instinctively realize how very important closeness, intimacy, and sharing are to her. What she needs most is just someone to listen.

By sharing her feelings, she begins to remember that she is worthy of love and that her needs will be fulfilled. Doubt and mistrust melt away. Her tendency to feel overly responsible and burdened relaxes as she remembers that she is worthy of love—she doesn't have to earn it; she can relax, give less, and receive more. She deserves it.

⪼⪻

Moving in the Right Direction

*T*o experience increasing fulfillment, a woman does not have to have all of her needs met at once. The whole process of dating is a gradual process of satisfying her needs a little at a time. To be satisfied, a woman just needs to feel hope that one day her emotional needs will be met. In a similar manner, a man doesn't have to have all his sexual needs met right away; he just needs the hope that they are moving in that direction.

> **To be satisfied, both men and women**
> **just need to know that they are moving toward getting**
> **what they want.**

When a man moves into a woman's world and expresses his support, she appreciates his willingness to help as much as the help itself. On an emotional level, she suddenly feels she is not as alone in the world. When a man does something concrete and tangible for a woman, not only does the woman feel supported but the man gets to feel successful. They both feel encouraged and reassured that they are moving together in the right direction.

✥✥

Asking for What You Want

A woman's biggest mistake in a relationship is to give up communicating her needs and start doing everything by herself. In the short term this is easier, but in the long run she is not developing the necessary communication and understanding in her relationship. Ultimately she will feel a consuming compulsion to do everything while wrongly assuming that her partner doesn't care to help or participate.

Women don't realize that men need to be asked for their help. Just as women resist having to ask for help, men may resist offering to help unless they are asked. Quite often men are not even resisting; their tunnel vision prevents them from recognizing how they are needed. Once they are asked, it is normal for them to work though some resistance to helping out. By simply ignoring this resistance, a woman can most successfully involve her partner once again in the relationship.

Women often misinterpret their partner's resistance to helping out.

If she persists in communicating, she can help a man become aware of her needs, which his tunnel vision prevents him from seeing. Tunnel vision is like a spell that can take over a man. He is released from that spell when he is able to hear the needs of others. When he is not mistrusted and rejected for his tunnel vision but loved, trusted, and talked to in a positive way, he can come back to his caring self. This kind of loving communication frees him from the spell.

Transformation is possible. By accepting and understanding each other's differences with love, our relationships can be transformed. We become more of who we truly are: loving and caring beings.

MARCH 28

The Self-Assured Woman

*S*ome women are naturally self-assured. They are born with this attitude, just as some singers are born with an incredible voice. For most, this attitude needs to be developed and cultivated. It is already inside a woman; it just needs the opportunity to come out and be exercised. By becoming aware of how it looks and feels, a woman can begin to find it and give expression to this part of herself.

A self-assured attitude needs to be practiced and cultivated.

Self-assurance is an attitude that assumes you will always get what you need and that at this moment you are in the process of getting it. Self-assurance assumes that others are available and want to help and that you don't have to do it all by yourself.

Self-assurance is different from confidence. When a woman is too confident and independent, it is sometimes a sign that she is not at all sure that others are there for her, and so she has to do it all herself. By focusing on cultivating an attitude of self-assurance, a woman can begin to open up to others for their support and not isolate herself.

MARCH 29

~~~

How We Lose the Attraction

To whatever extent a partner must suppress their way of being, feeling, thinking, and doing to receive love or be safe in a relationship, the passion will fade.

As we conform or reform, not only do we lessen the passion but we also diminish the love.

Every time you suppress, repress, or deny yourself in order to be loved, you are not loving yourself. You are giving yourself the message that you are not good enough the way you are. Every time you try to alter, fix, or improve your partner, you are sending them the message that they do not deserve to be loved for who they are.

Under these conditions, love dies. Trying to preserve the magic of love by conforming or reforming, we only make matters worse. When, in the name of love, we seek to repress ourselves or change our partner, that is actually a kind of dysfunctional love. Healthy love is free and seeks to nurture our partners in being true to themselves. It is never an act of love if we have to give up an essential part of who we are in giving to another.

Understanding our differences frees us to be less judgmental and more accepting. From this loving perspective, we can be more successful in finding creative solutions and compromises that allow us to be ourselves and support our partners in being themselves while not sacrificing what we need.

MARCH 30

When to Talk About Sex

*Q*uite often it is just not romantic to ask a woman what she wants while you are having sex. It is best done either after sex or at another time when you are not immediately planning to have sex. During sex, she doesn't want to think about her needs. Instead, she wants to feel more and let it all gradually unfold.

To gather information about what a woman likes in bed, a man should listen carefully to how she responds during sex. A man needs to hear a woman verbally express her pleasure. That way he gets the feedback he needs to know what is working to fulfill her. A woman may even enjoy sex more when she expresses her feelings verbally.

What Makes a Man Listen

A woman's attitude has the power to turn a man on or to turn him off. A man will most respect and want to hear what a woman has to say when she speaks in a manner that first assumes he is interested. The very act of assuming that a man will be interested makes him more interested. Even if he wasn't that interested in the subject matter, he will become interested because he is interested in her. It is all in her approach.

> ***A woman needs to remember that she is the jewel,***
> ***and the man provides the setting for her to shine.***

If her attitude says she feels assured that he will be interested, then he will want to hear her and know her. Self-assurance draws a man's interest. A woman needs to remember that she is the jewel, and he is providing the setting for her to shine. As long as he gets credit for making her shine, he is happy to be the provider of support in the relationship. The attitude that she is already worthy of attention makes her more desirable and intriguing to him.

❧ APRIL ❧

Passion, Courage, Forgiveness

*I*n the month of April, all things seem possible—even forgiveness. With the courage to forgive, we can rediscover our passion. As you work through your feelings in a caring and constructive manner, as you learn to release yourself from negativity, you will feel a resurgence of positive emotions. These emotions reignite the passion that lovers share for each other.

When you hold onto your anger and resentment, it is you who misses out on love. Find the courage to release your negative feelings, and you'll discover that genuine state of love and forgiveness that is so essential to creating a lifetime of love. It takes courage to love, but it is worth it. The greatest tragedy in life is not the loss of love but those who do not open their hearts to love again.

~~~~~~

Apologies and Forgiveness

A relationship thrives when a man focuses on correcting his behavior to be more considerate and the woman focuses on correcting her attitude toward his mistakes. In an environment of acceptance and forgiveness, a man is more motivated to acknowledge his mistakes and grow through self-correction.

When one partner apologizes, that makes it easier for the other to find forgiveness. When one partner is very forgiving, that makes it easy for the other to be more responsible and to apologize. It is difficult for a man to apologize for his mistakes when he does not sense that he will be forgiven. It is equally difficult for a woman to forgive a man's mistakes when he does not apologize. One cannot exist for long without the other.

Apologies and forgiveness are interdependent.

A man's ability to self-correct depends on how accepted he feels. When a man feels punished by his partner, it is difficult for him to become more considerate and sensitive to her needs. When men can apologize, not only are women happier but the man also gets what he needs most—her trust, acceptance, and appreciation.

By practicing forgiveness, a woman discovers her power to bring out the best in a man and herself. By finding the forgiving part in herself, a woman will connect with her most loving self. By taking the risk to forgive, a woman unlocks the door to her heart.

APRIL 2

Giving Up Blame

*W*hen a woman realizes she has been giving too much, she tends to blame her partner for their unhappiness. She feels the injustice of giving more than she has received. She feels resentful.

Although she has not received what she deserved, to improve her relationships she needs to recognize how she contributed to the problem. When a woman gives too much, she should not blame her partner. Similarly, a man who gives less should not blame his partner for being negative or unreceptive to him. In both cases, blaming does not work.

Understanding, trust, compassion, acceptance, and support are the solution, not blaming our partner. Instead of blaming his partner for being resentful, a man can be compassionate and offer his support, even if she doesn't ask for it; listen to her, even if at first it sounds like blame; and help her to trust and open up to him by doing little things for her to show that he cares.

Instead of blaming a man for giving less, a woman needs to accept and forgive her partner's imperfections, trust that he wants to give more even when he doesn't offer his support, and encourage him to give more by continuing to ask for his support and appreciating what he does give.

A woman needs to remember that she doesn't have to give more to make a relationship work. As a man experiences her limits, he is actually motivated to give more. When she respects her limits, he is automatically motivated to question the effectiveness of his behavior patterns and to start making changes. When a woman realizes that in order to receive she needs to set limits, she automatically begins to forgive her partner and explore new ways of asking for and receiving support. When a woman sets limits, she gradually learns to relax and receive more.

APRIL 3

Women and Sex

*W*omen today expect more from sex than ever before. It used to be that sex was primarily a way a woman fulfilled her husband. For many of our mothers, sex was something she did for him and not for herself. Now that birth control is more reliable and available, and society is much more accepting of women's sexual needs and desires, women have greater permission to explore and enjoy their sensual side. For many women, a growing interest in sex also reflects their need to find balance within themselves by reconnecting with their feminine side.

Having spent most of the day in a traditionally male job, she too wants a "wife" to greet her with love when she gets home. She too wants to enjoy the release that sex brings. Great sex fulfills her as much as it fulfills him. To cope with the stress of the modern workplace, not only does he need her support but she needs his as well. By learning new relationship skills, men and women can solve this problem together.

> ***Great sex fulfills her as much as it fulfills him.***

Great sex softens a woman and opens her to experience the love in her heart and to remember her partner's love for her in a most definite way. Her partner's skillful and knowing touch leaves no doubt in her mind that she is important to him. The hunger for love within her soul is fulfilled with her partner's passionate and fully present attention. An ever-present tension is momentarily released as she surrenders once again to the deepest longings of her feminine being. Her passion to love and be loved can be fully felt and fulfilled.

April 4

The Soul Mate Challenge

If your life partner did not challenge you in some ways, the best would not be drawn from you. Soul mates are the perfect partners to bring out the best in us, and sometimes that is done by having to work through issues. In a marriage, you have to overcome all kinds of negative tendencies—being too judgmental, critical, selfish, compliant, demanding, needy, rigid, accommodating, righteous, doubtful, impatient, and so on.

A soul mate is not perfect, but perfect for you.

A soul mate gives you the opportunity to rise above these tendencies. When your dark side surfaces, you become stronger and more loving by exercising the love you feel deep in your heart to resolve an issue. In this process your soul, like the butterfly, has a chance to fly free.

APRIL 5

Sex at Its Best

*S*ex is great when it is shared in love and the love keeps growing. For a woman to grow in sexual fulfillment, she primarily needs to feel emotionally supported in the relationship, but it is also important for the man to understand her different sexual needs.

For a man to grow in sexual fulfillment, he primarily needs to feel successful in fulfilling his partner sexually. This requires that he practice new skills not only in the relationship but also in bed.

When You Suppress Your Feelings

*N*ot telling the truth about your feelings in a relationship is like not watering a plant—you end up killing something that once was alive and growing. The inevitable result of holding back the truth from someone you care for is that you hold back the love as well. After some time in a relationship in which the truth is not expressed, you will look back and wonder, "What happened to that juicy feeling? Where did the magic go?" The answer is that the love and magic are buried under piles of uncommunicated emotions.

You simply cannot repress your negative feelings (anger, sadness, fear, and sorrow) and expect the positive emotions to remain lively. When you numb yourself to your undesirable emotions, you are numbing your ability to feel positive emotions as well.

Suppressing negative feelings suppresses positive feelings as well.

The long-term effects of not telling the truth to yourself and others and of pushing down your feelings is that you lose your ability to feel positive emotions like joy, excitement, and passion. The dictionary defines passion as "an intense feeling." Every time you suppress a feeling you don't want to deal with, you are systematically limiting your ability to feel. Step by step you are killing the passion in all of your relationships.

Advanced Bedroom Skills

*M*ore and more, men and women would rather get a divorce than stay in a passionless marriage. Neither sex is willing to put up with the old system of a man having discreet affairs to fulfill his sexual passion while a woman sacrifices her need for passion in favor of maintaining the family unit. AIDS and other sexually transmitted diseases make extramarital affairs far more dangerous than they were in the past.

A modern man wants his partner to value sex in a way that allows him to stay passionately connected to her and their relationship. To achieve this end, advanced bedroom skills are required for both men and women. A woman cannot remain passionate toward her partner unless she feels cherished and special. A man cannot remain passionate unless he feels his partner is equally interested in having sex.

꙳꙳꙳

Releasing Your Negative Feelings

*T*he process of releasing your negative feelings and coming to a genuine state of love and forgiveness is essential for your personal growth. When you stop loving, it is you who suffers the most. When you hold on to anger and resentment, it is you who misses out on love. When you are willing to work through your negative emotions to your willingness to love, you are the one who is the winner.

By giving yourself permission to feel and heal your negative emotions, you allow the obstructed love inside to flow again. Expressing the negative feelings that come up in a relationship is not a sign of weakness or failure. On the contrary, it is a sign of strength that you are committed to resolving whatever negative emotions get in the way of your feeling in love all the time.

꠸꠸꠸

Keeping the Passion Alive

*W*hen partners are able to keep their differences alive by loving and respecting each other, they can sustain the passion in their relationship. When men and women become too similar, they lose the attraction or chemistry. It is boring to be with someone just like yourself. To maintain passion in a relationship, we must work to preserve our differences while gradually incorporating the qualities of our partner.

Passion in the beginning of a relationship generally tells us that what we are attracted to in our partner is also latent within ourselves. If we are attracted to our mate's warmth, then that very warmth is seeking to emerge from our potential or unconscious self, to be integrated into our conscious being. Our strong attraction arises from our need to feel whole and complete within ourselves. As we love each other, we have the opportunity to grow together and keep the passion alive for a lifetime.

In the Bedroom
Women Are Like the Moon,
Men Are Like the Sun

*I*n the bedroom, a woman's sexual experience is always waxing or waning. A woman is like the moon. Sometimes she is like the full moon, but at other times she is like the new moon. At the new moon or even the half moon, regardless of what a great lover her partner is, she will not have an orgasm. Yet even though she is unable to have an orgasm, sex is still satisfying to her.

A man is different in this respect. He is like the sun, which rises every morning with a big smile. If a man is aroused enough to have sex, then he is generally not satisfied if he doesn't have an orgasm.

A man's sexuality is like the sun,
which rises every morning with a smile.

A woman's sexual cycle tends to last approximately twenty-eight days. Sometimes she is in the full moon stage of her cycle, sometimes in the half moon stage, and sometimes in the new moon stage. In each of these phases and all the phases in between, her sexual longings will vary. There is no way to predict which stage she is in. Even from month to month, the length of the cycle varies.

For a woman, an orgasm, or full moon sex, is like going to a fireworks display, while sex at the half moon is like the pleasure of a picnic lunch on a beautiful spring day. Even sex at the new moon is satisfying in a different way. It is like waking up after a great sleep. She still feels really good that he had his orgasm. A man needs to remember that a woman doesn't require an orgasm every time to be satisfied.

Unless a man understands this difference, he will think something is wrong when his partner doesn't have an orgasm, and he will eventually lose interest. A man needs to understand that for a woman orgasm is not the main goal. She can enjoy the closeness and affection or simply his passionate desire just as much as an orgasm.

APRIL 11

~~~~~

When Questions Are a Turnoff

*A*sking a man a series of questions about why he is not in the mood is not only an immediate turnoff but can prevent his being in the mood in the future. Here are some questions not to ask if he doesn't respond to your sexually inviting signals.

"You used to always want sex. What's wrong?"

"Don't you want to have sex with me anymore?"

"Do you think I am getting fat?"

"Are you still attracted to me?"

"Aren't you turned on to me?"

"Do you still love me? Maybe we should talk about it."

"Are we ever going to have sex again? Maybe we should get some help."

"You were looking at other women tonight. Don't you want to be with me anymore?"

"Would you rather be with someone else?"

"Did I do something to turn you off?"

"Why don't you want to have sex?"

Certainly there may be appropriate times to ask these questions, but they are definitely not recommended when you have just undressed in front of him and he is tired and turning away from you. By being neutral and indirect, you can successfully convey the nondemanding message that you would welcome him if he happens to be in the mood.

Why Sex Is So Important

*W*e're all aware that sex tends to be more important to men while romance is more important to women, but we generally don't understand why. Without a deeper understanding of this fundamental difference, women commonly underestimate the importance of sex for men and many times judge them as superficial for wanting only one thing.

A woman's judgments begin to soften when she discovers the real reasons that some men seem to want only sex. With a deeper understanding of our sexual differences based on our historical development and social conditioning, she can begin to understand why, for many men, sexual arousal is the key for helping them connect with and realize their loving feelings.

It is through sex that a man's heart opens, allowing him to experience both his loving feelings and his hunger for love as well. Ironically, it is sex that allows a man to feel his need for love, while it is receiving love that helps a woman to feel her hunger for sex.

APRIL 13

~~~~~~~

How to Avoid Arguments

*T*he secret to loving and respectful communication is avoiding painful arguments. The differences and disagreements that inevitably come up in a relationship don't hurt as much as the ways in which we communicate them. Ideally, an argument does not have to be hurtful. It can simply be an engaging conversation that expresses our differences and disagreements.

Practically speaking, most couples start out arguing about one thing and, within five minutes, are arguing about the way they are arguing. Unknowingly they begin hurting each other. What could have been an innocent argument, easily resolved with mutual understanding and an acceptance of differences, escalates into a battle.

> ***In painful arguments we refuse***
> ***to accept or understand our partner's point of view***
> ***because of the way we are being approached.***

Resolving an argument requires extending or stretching our point of view to include and integrate another point of view. To make this stretch, we need to feel appreciated and respected. If our partner's attitude is unloving, our self-esteem can actually be wounded by taking on their point of view.

The more intimate we are with others, the more difficult it is to hear their point of view objectively without reacting to negative feelings. To protect ourselves from feeling worthy of their disrespect or disapproval, automatic defenses come up to resist their point of view. Even if we agree with their point of view, we may stubbornly persist in arguing with them. Slowing down and taking time to listen first will always pave the way for our partner to hear us.

APRIL 14

He Wants to Sleep on It, but She Doesn't

*T*he old advice that warns couples never to go to bed upset or angry can make a lot of trouble today. When a man is angry, I recommend that a woman give him lots of space and let him sleep on it. Wait till he has cooled off a bit before talking together about what is bothering him.

If a woman is upset and a man is centered enough to listen without getting upset, then it is advisable for him to initiate a conversation, ask questions, and draw her out by making it safe for her to talk. The old adage about not going to bed angry was mainly for men to understand about women. A woman didn't need to apply it because when her husband was upset he usually went off to deal with his feelings alone.

Men today are more in touch with their female tendencies. When they are upset or angry, they sometimes want to talk. It is important for women to understand the wisdom of postponing these kinds of conversations, particularly if you have previously had negative and painful arguments.

APRIL 15

Sex and Passion

*W*ithout passion, sex becomes routine and boring. With love and the assistance of advanced bedroom skills, a couple can continue to experience great passion and fulfillment. Instead of becoming less passionate over the years, a man who sees and touches his wife's naked body can be more turned on than ever.

Not only can he be excited by the pleasure of arousal and increasing sexual intensity, but he can also be aware of how much more love, warmth, passion, and sensual affection he will be able to experience as well as provide for her. This awareness elevates sex to an even higher level of passion and excitement.

When she feels his passion for her, she can rejoice in his continued desire to connect with her and provide her with pleasure. The wise woman recognizes sex as an opportunity to share love in a way that nurtures him the most. Sex becomes a beautiful expression of her love for him and an opportunity to receive in the deepest fibers of her femininity his love for her.

Sex and Decision Making

Sex is one area in relationships where the decision-making process is particularly important. Generally a man knows when he is open to having sex. A woman may be open to having sex but may need more time to discover whether she really wants to. Men don't understand this, because when they are open to having sex, they simultaneously want it.

When a husband asks his wife whether she would like to have sex that night, if she says, "I don't know," it is very easy for him to misinterpret and think she is saying no. Though he thinks he is being rejected, she is just warming up to the idea. She may be quite open to having sex but needs some time for her inner feelings to emerge before she can make the decision. With sex, as with many other areas of life, it is essential for men to understand that when a woman says, "I don't know," she is not saying no.

One way for him to be assured that he is not being rejected is to ask, after she says she doesn't know, "Is there a part of you that wants to have sex?" Almost always she will have a positive response. With this encouragement it is easy for him to then take the time to support her in exploring her feelings. Even if she eventually decides she is not in the mood, he doesn't feel so rejected.

APRIL 17

~~~

Passionate Monogamy

*A*lthough women need romance to feel loved, for passion to grow over time their most important intimacy requirement is monogamy. A man can make the romantic gestures, but if he is not monogamous, her passion cannot grow. Romance tells a woman that she is special. And there is nothing that makes a woman feel more special than a man in touch with his passions and wanting only her.

As a woman ages, her ability to feel and express passion increases if she feels she can fully trust her partner to be there for her. If she feels she is being compared with another woman or that she has to compete, she cannot continue to open up.

If she senses that he is having an affair or could have an affair, she may shut down. She needs the clear and clean water of monogamy to gradually unfold, one petal at a time, like a delicate rose.

Not only does she benefit from monogamy, but he does too! When a man is trusted by his wife and family, others sense something they can trust about him. Sexual monogamy strengthens a man and makes him worthy of the highest trust.

APRIL 18

What Drives a Man

*T*he strongest drive in a man is the desire to please a woman. This willful desire gives him power. It first manifests as the sex drive. Later, as he is able to blend it with the desire to love and respect, understand, and care for a woman, it becomes even more powerful. When a man expresses his love physically, emotionally, mentally, and spiritually, then his power is at maximum.

APRIL 19

Great Sex

*L*ike a fabulous vacation after working hard, or a sensual walk through the forest on a sunny spring day, or the exhilaration of climbing to the top of a mountain, great sex is not just a reward but something that can rejuvenate the body, mind, and soul. It brightens our days and strengthens our relationship in the most basic ways.

A great sex life is not just the symptom of a passionate relationship but a major factor in creating it. Great sex fills our hearts with love and can fulfill almost all our emotional needs. Loving sex, passionate sex, sensual sex, tender sex, rough sex, soft sex, hard sex, romantic sex, goal-oriented sex, erotic sex, simple sex, cool sex, and hot sex are all an important part of keeping the passion of love alive.

APRIL 20

Women and Quickies

During sex, if a woman begins to realize that she is not going to have an orgasm, instead of continuing to try, she can say, "Let's just have a quickie." This little phrase can make a world of difference. He has no problem shifting from trying to give her an orgasm to going for his own orgasm.

Just as a man needs to take a long time
for a woman to be fulfilled in sex,
sometimes he needs her to not take a long time.

Her not having an orgasm is only difficult when they don't share an understanding that he has not failed her. When she says, "Let's just have a quickie," a part of him feels relieved. It reminds him that it is not his fault or hers; it is just not the time for her to have an orgasm. He can successfully fulfill her just by being affectionate and holding her while he goes for it.

❦

Creating Healthy Intimacy

*T*he real joy of a special, intimate, and committed relationship is the opportunity to share and celebrate the good times and give to your partner when they are in need. When you are in need and your partner is not giving to you, you can safely assume that they are also in need and thus are unable to support you.

It is unhealthy to depend too much on our partner.

It is unrealistic to depend on our intimate partner to heal us when we are out of balance. They are sometimes capable of this but not always. When we start to depend on others to heal us, fix us, or change us, then we make it even more difficult for them to support us.

Understanding our differing stress reactions gives us a constructive approach for healing ourselves or for reaching out to others for help in healing ourselves. The bonus is that when we succeed in finding balance, we know the correct strategies for supporting our partner.

APRIL 22

✦

Writing a Sex Letter

Domestic stresses can easily overshadow and lessen sexual feelings. The sexual feelings may be inside us, but they need a little extra help to come out in the home. If you find that when you are away from your partner you are getting turned on, but when you are home you are not turned on, practice writing down your sexual feelings when they arise.

In a letter to your partner, express what you want to do. Describe the scene and your feelings as if it is really happening. Of course, many people are not writers, and expressing these delicate sentiments may be difficult. That does not mean the feelings don't exist; it just means that you are not gifted in expressing them in words. Women particularly love to hear these emotions in words. That is one reason women spend billions of dollars buying romance novels.

A man who has difficulty verbalizing his passion might want to buy a greeting card that poetically expresses how he feels. It is perfectly normal to have loving feelings and not know how to articulate them in a way that does them justice. Picking the right card to express your feelings is just as good as writing the words yourself.

APRIL 23

~~~~~

Complementary Needs

*S*oul mates basically have something that their partners need. When a man has what a woman needs, she feels chemistry. For men, it is the other way around. When a woman needs what a man has to offer, he feels chemistry. This mutual dependence creates healthy emotional chemistry.

Emotional chemistry frees us from being limited by our unrealistic pictures of what our ideal partner will look like or be like. When a man is able to experience the thrill of feeling needed by a woman, he is no longer caught in pictures and expectations of what his ideal partner should look like. He is released from judging her physical appearance when he enjoys the pleasure of making little romantic gestures and feeling her response.

Similarly, when a woman experiences a man treating her in a special way, she is free from fixating on how her ideal partner should look. By experiencing chemistry that results from being receptive to a man's approach, she is free to follow her heart and not get caught up in unrealistic expectations of perfection.

*One Secret to Making a Woman
Feel Loved*

*P*ossibly the most important way a man can make a woman feel loved is completely the opposite of what most men think. Most men unconsciously think that if they don't complain about the relationship, their partners will feel loved and valued. After all, if a woman doesn't complain about him, he will feel appreciated. Men don't understand that when he acts as though everything is fine in the relationship, his partner infers that the relationship is not important to him, which makes her feel as though she is not important to him.

Generally, a man tends to get upset and worry most about problems at work. When he comes home, his mind is still on his job. His partner gets the message that work is more important to him than she is. If this man can learn to identify and share some of his frustrations, disappointments, and worries in the relationship, he will communicate to the woman that she is important, appreciated, and needed.

~≈≈~

The Seven Secrets of Lasting Passion

*T*o sustain passion in a relationship, there are seven important secret areas. They are as follows:

1. *Differences attract*—Accept the differences and love can grow. *Vivent les différences.*

2. *Change and growth*—To stay interested and interesting we must continue to grow and change. Don't deny your true self.

3. *Feelings, needs, and vulnerability*—Stay in touch with your feelings and continue to ask for what you need.

4. *Personal responsibility and self-healing*—As you grow in love, old unresolved feelings come up to be healed. Whenever we are blaming our partner, we really need to go deeper into ourselves and heal our past.

5. *Love, romance, and monogamy*—Lasting passion is not automatic. We need to apply ourselves to create romantic opportunities for her to feel cherished and for him to feel successful.

6. *Friendship, autonomy, and fun*—A relationship should not be all work or too serious. There needs to be space to forgive all mistakes and have fun. Create fun opportunities to let go of the past and joyfully be in the present.

7. *Partnership and service to a higher purpose*—Make sure that a part of your life together is dedicated to fulfilling some cause outside yourself.

APRIL 26

Communication Is for Women What Sex Is for Men

*J*ust as communication is important to a woman, sexual gratification is important to a man. He needs constant reassurance that his partner likes sex with him. Sexual rejection is traumatic to a man's sense of self.

I'm not saying that a woman should feel obliged to have sex whenever her partner wants it. I am saying that she needs to work hard to be hypersensitive when sex is the subject under discussion. If he initiates sex and she's not into it, she shouldn't just say no. Instead, say "A part of me wants to have sex, but I think I would enjoy it more later."

By considering his feelings, she frees him to continue initiating sex without feeling rejected. Or she may say, "I'm not really in the mood for sex, but we could have a quickie."

Just as communication is the primary means for a woman to experience love, sex is the primary way for a man to connect with love and passion on an ongoing basis.

~~~~~

How to Rekindle the Passion

*A*lthough as a general rule of thumb the relationship comes first before sex can be enjoyed, sometimes having loving sex can dramatically improve the relationship. A woman's willingness to have sex can open up a man's love for her. Sometimes even if she is feeling cold, having sex with him and feeling his love for her can begin to open her up again.

Perhaps the partners are simply out of the habit of having sex regularly. Outside the home they are free to feel their sexual desires, but in the home the old routine of not having sex takes over. Once sex gets put on the back burner it becomes harder to bring back without advanced relationship skills. With a greater awareness of what skills are needed, even when the passion is gone, it is often very easy to rekindle.

APRIL 28

Healing Repressed Feelings

*A*n intimate relationship is the ideal setting for healing repressed feelings. When you find someone you feel safe with and loved by, all your repressed feelings gradually begin to surface in an attempt to be healed. Taking time to explore your feelings in a journal assists greatly in recognizing that often what you are upset about has more to do with your past than your present.

Through honest and loving personal relationships, you can not only learn to master the everyday tension that arises between you and another person but you can also use the relationship as an opportunity to heal old hurts, enabling you to become a more powerfully loving and lovable person.

When Her Pleasure Becomes His Pleasure

*T*he more emotionally connected to a woman a man is, the more her pleasure becomes his pleasure. By physically moving inside her being, he also emotionally moves inside her and can actually experience her fulfillment as his own.

If a woman has a great time, the man tends to take credit for it, and it excites him even more. His fulfillment and pleasure are ensured by her fulfillment. Ultimately his fulfillment in sex is determined or measured by her maximum fulfillment. If she doesn't have an orgasm, he mistakenly thinks that she was not fulfilled. This tendency can be overcome when he understands that she can be just as fulfilled without always having an orgasm.

This understanding is such a relief for both partners. He can stop measuring the success of sex by her orgasms, and she can stop feeling the pressure to have an orgasm when her body is not responding in that way. Instead he can measure his success by her fulfillment, and she can relax and enjoy the sex without the pressure.

It's Not Your Fault

*T*he more a woman practices preparing a man before sharing in conversation, the less she will need to prepare him in the future. As with the acquisition of any new skill, it is wise to begin with easy problems and then graduate to difficult ones. A woman's start-up assistance makes it easier for a man.

When a woman is upset, she can prepare a man to listen by simply saying, "I want you to know that you don't have to fix anything or change in any way. I just need to share my feelings and then I will feel much better." When a man is not concerned with having to defend his actions or plan a solution to her feelings, he is free to really hear what she is saying.

> ***As a man begins to understand, his actions***
> ***will automatically be more considerate.***

Not only can she prepare him for listening, but if she notices that her man is getting frustrated or angry while she is talking, she can pause for a moment and say something like "I know this sounds like blame but it is not. You are not responsible for how I feel. I really appreciate your listening. It helps me to feel better." Then she can resume sharing her feelings. In this way, by releasing a man from feeling as if it is all his fault, she ensures that he can hear her better.

⋙ MAY ⋘

Harmony, Diversity, Appreciation

*M*ay is a month to appreciate the harmony you and your partner enjoy despite your diversity as individuals. Harmony and diversity are necessary ingredients for the success of any long-term relationship.

So often we enter into a relationship attracted by those things that make us different, and soon we are bent upon changing one another. We can easily fall into the trap of resenting, resisting, and ultimately rejecting each other's differences: men expect women to think and react like men, and women expect men to feel and behave like women.

Real love, though, is unconditional. It does not demand but affirms and values. Despite the fact that you differ, as all men and women do, you also share and cherish many common goals. Family, work, religion, politics, money, character, recreation, sex—all the values that resonate inside you—are among the things that create the harmony you sense between you and your partner.

Whatever those common goals are, you cannot allow yourself to forget that love is accepting and appreciating a person not just when they meet our expectations but also when they don't.

MAY 1

Resonance

*S*oul mates have similar values that resonate. This element of chemistry inspires us to be the best we can be. When we are with our partner, what is most important to them resonates with what is really important to us.

Your partner's values concerning God, family, work, recreation, politics, money, character, sex, and marriage resonate with you and inspire you. You are able to see the good in your soul mate and respect and admire their values. To have similar values does not mean that you will necessarily think and feel the same way about issues, but you will be able to respect your partner's viewpoint and admire where they are coming from.

MAY 2

People Are Different

*P*eople are different. Recognizing this fundamental truth is essential for creating positive and loving relationships. Unnecessary problems and conflict arise when we do not fully acknowledge that people differ from us. When we forget that we are supposed to be different and that differences are okay, we become bent upon changing one another.

We resent, resist, and reject each other's differences. We demand that the people in our lives feel, think, and behave as we would. When they react differently, we make them wrong or invalidate them; we try to fix them when they really need understanding and nurturing. We try to improve them when they need acceptance, appreciation, and trust.

We unknowingly demand that the people in our lives feel, think, and behave as we would.

We complain that if only they would change, we could love them; if only they would agree, we could love them; if only they would feel the way we do, we could love them; if only they would do what we ask, we could love them.

What then is love? Is love accepting and appreciating a person only when they fulfill our expectations? Is love the act of changing a person into what we want rather than what they choose to be? Is love caring for or trusting a person because they think and feel the way we do?

Certainly this is not love. It may feel like love to the giver but not to the receiver. Real love is unconditional. It does not demand but affirms and values. Unconditional love is not possible without the recognition and acceptance of our differences. As long as we mistakenly believe that our loved ones would be better off thinking, feeling, and behaving the way we do, true love is obstructed. Once we realize that not only are people different but they are supposed to be that way, the obstacles to real love begin to fall away.

MAY 3

Everyone Is Special

*E*very one of us is born with a unique and special value. There is no one who can be a better you. You have a special place in this universe. A part of growing up is discovering your own niche—finding out what you have to offer, what you are here to do, and then doing it. This discovery will bring you deep fulfillment and enliven the core of your being. The only way to accomplish this task is to stop masking who you really are and to begin accepting and loving yourself the way you are.

≈≈≈

Good Intentions Are Not Enough

*F*alling in love is always magical. It feels eternal, as if love will last forever. We naively believe that somehow we are exempt from the problems our parents had, free from the odds that love will die, assured that it is meant to be and that we are destined to live happily ever after.

As the magic recedes and daily life takes over, it emerges that men continue to expect women to think and react like men, and women expect men to feel and behave like women. Without a clear awareness of our differences, we do not take the time to understand and respect each other. We become demanding, resentful, judgmental, and intolerant.

With the best and most loving intentions, love continues to die. Somehow problems creep in. Resentments build. Communication breaks down. Mistrust increases. Rejection and repression result. The magic of love is lost. Very few people indeed are able to grow in love. Yet it does happen.

When men and women are able to respect and accept their differences, then love has a chance to blossom.

By understanding the hidden differences of the opposite sex, we can more successfully give and receive the love that is in our hearts.

By validating and accepting our differences, creative solutions can be discovered whereby we can succeed in getting what we want. And, more importantly, we can learn how best to love and support the people we care about. Love is magical, and it can last, if we remember our differences.

MAY 5

Soul Mates Are Not Perfect

*A*n important insight about your soul mate is that they are never perfect. They will not have everything on your list of ideal qualities. They come with baggage. They, like you, have good days and bad days. They may not look the way you thought they would look; they may have flaws that you don't like very much. They are not perfect, but when your heart is open and you know them, they are somehow perfect for you.

The love you spontaneously feel for a soul mate is the foundation for learning to share your life with someone who in many ways is very different from you. That love motivates you to cooperate, respect, appreciate, cherish, and admire that person. In this process, which is not always easy or comfortable, you become a better person. Your soul has a chance to grow.

MAY 6

What Women Admire in Men

A woman admires a man if he has the strength to control his emotions and the sensitivity to consider the merits and validity of what she is saying. He doesn't have to put his tail between his legs and do whatever she wants.

Women are turned off by passive and submissive men. They don't want to be the boss in an intimate relationship. They want to be equal partners. If a man respects a woman's primary need to be heard, she will respond by becoming equally respectful of his wishes.

MAY 7

How a Man Thrives

A man thrives when he feels that he does not have to give but that he chooses to give. He wants to give because he cares and it makes a woman happy—not because he owes her. Expectations are a turnoff.

When a man feels he has to give because a woman has given so much to him, then it is no longer fun to give. It is like working to pay off your debts. A woman loses her sense of receptivity when she expects more than a man has been giving.

It is fine to expect a man's support if he has been giving it consistently over time, but this kind of expectation is different because it is based on past experience, not just on an assumption.

MAY 8

~~~~~

Fear of Being Different

*O*ne of the reasons we fail to acknowledge our differences is that while we were growing up, being different meant being laughed at or rejected. To become popular or powerful, we needed to become like those who were already popular or powerful. As kids, we spent a lot of time trying to be like other kids.

Even though we are adults now, and even if we were very fortunate in having parents who supported us in our uniqueness, we are still apt to think that being different means risking rejection and failure.

How Sex Is Different for Men and Women

*S*ex is a very different experience for women and men. A man experiences pleasure primarily as a release of sexual tension. A woman experiences sex in the opposite way. For her the great joys of sex correspond to a gradual buildup of tension. The more she can feel her desire for sex, the more fulfilling it is.

For a man, sex instinctively is a testosterone drive toward the ultimate release of climax. When he becomes aroused, he automatically seeks release. His fulfillment in sex is mainly associated with the release of tension leading to and including the orgasm.

Biologically, in a man's body there is an inner sac of semen already waiting and seeking release, unlike a woman, whose fluids are generated through arousal. When a man is aroused, he is already seeking release. In a sense, he is trying to empty out while she is seeking to be filled up.

A man's immediate desire to be touched in his sensitive zones is a given. He does not need much help in getting excited. He needs help in releasing or letting go of his excitement. In a sense, he seeks to end his excitement, while a woman seeks to extend her excitement to feel her inner longing more deeply.

She relishes his ability to slowly build up her desire to be touched in her most sensitive zones. As one layer at a time is stripped away, she longs for the deeper layers of her sensual soul to be revealed. As much as he wants immediate satisfaction of his desire for sexual stimulation, she hungers and loves to feel her desire increase.

May 10

Balancing the Masculine and the Feminine

*I*ronically, men go out of balance because they are not getting the support from women they used to get in the old days, while women go out of balance because they are not getting a new kind of support from men.

To solve our modern problems, women need to find within themselves the feminine love they used to share but without giving up the new power they are expressing. A modern man's challenge is to draw upon his ancient courage and risk failure by trying out new formulas for success in order to support the woman he loves in new ways. He must learn to be keep his strength and confidence as he becomes more sensitive and considerate of others and their needs.

MAY 11

~~~~

Appreciation Is Contagious

*A*t times you may feel that your partner doesn't appreciate you. Some people decide that if they are not getting enough love, they would rather leave than ask for it. They think to themselves, "I don't want to beg for love." But asking for what you want is not begging. If you aren't getting the love and appreciation you want, it's your responsibility to ask for it. Assume that your partner wants to support you and only needs some guidance from you. You don't have to wait for compliments or fish for them. You deserve to be appreciated.

Try spending a few moments at the end of each day appreciating each other for all you have done. Take turns saying, "Something I appreciate about you is. . . ." Let your partner know some of the things you feel you should be appreciated for by saying, "Something you should appreciate me for is . . ."

Remember, appreciation is a two-way street. If you are sitting around waiting for your partner or your friends to appreciate you, stop to ask yourself if you have been expressing your appreciation for them. Appreciation is contagious. The more you express your gratitude for others, the safer they will feel in expressing their gratitude for you. Tell your partner why you love them, not just that you love them. No one ever gets tired of hearing all the reasons they are loved. Be specific—that will give meaning and significance to your love.

MAY 12

~~~~~

Remembering Our Differences

*W*ithout the awareness that we are supposed to be different, men and women are at odds with each other. We usually become angry or frustrated with the opposite sex because we have forgotten this important truth. We expect the opposite sex to be more like ourselves. We desire them to want what we want and feel the way we feel.

We mistakenly assume that if our partners love us, they will react and behave in certain ways—the ways we react and behave when we love someone. This attitude sets us up to be disappointed again and again and prevents us from taking the necessary time to communicate lovingly about our differences.

> ***We mistakenly assume that if our partners love us,***
> ***they will react and behave the way we do.***

Men mistakenly expect women to think, communicate, and react the way men do; women mistakenly expect men to feel, communicate, and respond the way women do. We have forgotten that men and women are supposed to be different. As a result, our relationships are filled with unnecessary friction and conflict.

Clearly recognizing and respecting these differences dramatically reduces confusion when dealing with the opposite sex. When you remember that men are from Mars and women are from Venus, everything becomes easier.

MAY 13

Differences Are Magic

*J*ust like magnets, differences in people attract. As we grow in understanding, we can begin to appreciate these differences. Differences become a problem when we don't take time to understand their validity. Without this insight we become afraid and mistakenly assume that our partner is just too different for us ever to get what we want and need.

The true differences between men and women are actually complementary, giving each the opportunity to find balance. If I am overly aggressive, I may be attracted to someone who is more relaxed and receptive. By relating with this more relaxed person, I am able to connect with the more relaxed qualities in my unconscious. These relaxed and receptive qualities balance out, support, or complement my more developed aggressive qualities. In this manner, complementary differences are what draw us to each other and create the mysterious feelings of chemistry.

That Delicate Balance

*S*ex is a very delicate balance, and men are more vulnerable than women to an imbalance. If a man wants sex more than a woman does and can patiently persist in initiating sex respectfully, he will gradually win a woman over, and she will want to have sex.

When a woman consistently wants sex more than a man does and expresses her unhappy feelings about it, he can start to feel really turned off. He begins to feel as if he is obligated to have sex and has to perform for her.

When a woman wants sex most, she must be careful to communicate her desires without sounding too unhappy or demanding. One successful approach is to let him know that she will be pleasuring herself while he is drifting off to sleep and that if at any time he wants to join in, then he will be welcome, even if he wants to join at the very end to do the honors.

When a woman is sexually autonomous in this way and not needy or demanding, she is creating a welcome invitation for more sex.

～❦～

Love and Compatibility

*C*ompatibility means that you and your partner have similar dreams and goals and that you agree on the ways in which you want to achieve those goals, separately and together. It means that the way you enjoy living and being is very similar to the way your partner enjoys living and being. Every relationship should serve a purpose and have a direction. If two people are not going in the same direction and growing together, their love will be torn apart.

Compatibility doesn't mean that you and your partner are exactly alike. Differences create attraction. If both people in a relationship were identical, the relationship would soon become boring. If those differences are too great, they produce conflict and tension rather than stimulation and balance.

If two people are not compatible with each other, their relationship is destined to die. Love and compatibility must go hand in hand for a relationship to work and keep on working. In counseling couples, I have found that ten to twenty percent of marriages were incompatible to start with. The couple never felt out their similarities and differences long enough to see whether they could live together in peace and harmony.

When you and your partner are growing in the same direction and share a common vision, you will naturally complement each other. You will need each other to help you in your individual growth and to help make the whole complete. Feeling mutual need in a relationship creates passion and excitement. The first heat of passionate love is enticing, but a relationship must be based on mutual need if it is going to survive.

MAY 16

Give Trust, Not Advice

On Venus, it is considered a loving gesture to offer advice, but on Mars it is not. Women need to remember that Martians do not offer advice unless it is directly requested. On Mars, the way of showing love is to trust another Martian to solve his problems on his own.

This doesn't mean a woman has to squash her feelings. It's okay for her to feel frustrated or even angry, as long as she doesn't try to change him. Any attempt to change him is unsupportive and counterproductive.

When a woman loves a man, she often forms a home improvement commitment and targets him. She tries to change him or improve him. She thinks her attempts to change him are loving, but he feels controlled, manipulated, rejected, and unloved. He will stubbornly reject her because he feels she is rejecting him. When a woman tries to change a man, he is not getting the loving trust and acceptance he needs to change and grow. The more a woman tries to change a man, the more he resists.

> **The more a woman tries to change a man,
> the more he resists.**

The problem is that when a man resists her attempts to improve him, she misinterprets his response. She mistakenly thinks he is not willing to change, probably because he does not love her enough. The truth is that he is resistant to changing because he believes he is not being loved enough. When a man feels loved, trusted, accepted, and appreciated, he automatically begins to change, grow, and improve.

MAY 17

Two Steps Forward and Then Back Again

*W*hen a woman takes two steps back, her partner can take two steps forward, just like dance partners. When he takes two steps back, she can take two steps forward. This give-and-take is the basic rhythm of relationships.

At other times, they both pull back and then come back together. Every relationship has those times when both partners have little to give, and so they pull back to recharge.

While dancing, a woman gracefully swings into the man's arms, then spins away. In a successful relationship, this same pattern is expressed. A woman is happy to see her partner and moves into his arms. After pausing and preparing him, she spins out of his arms and shares her feelings in a circular manner.

At other times, he will hold her in his arms as she swings back and dips. In a similar way, as a woman shares her feelings she may dip. With his sympathetic support, she is able to go almost all the way down to the floor and then experience the joy of coming back up.

In dancing, a woman naturally spins around while the man stays steady. In a similar manner, when a woman can share her feelings without a man reacting with his, she can feel heard. Certainly there are also times when they both spin, but as in a dance, they need to pull away to do the movement before again making contact.

While dancing, a man gets to feel his sense of independence and autonomy by leading, and a woman gets to feel her need for cooperation and relationship by supporting him as he supports her in the moves she wants to make.

Women Expand, Men Contract

*O*ne of the most common problems women have in relationships is that they forget their own needs and become absorbed in the needs of their partner. A woman's greatest challenge in a relationship is to maintain her sense of self while she is expanding to serve the needs of others. In a complementary way, a man's biggest difficulty is to overcome his tendency to be self-absorbed and self-centered.

Women tend to expand; men tend to pull back or contract. Like centripetal force, men usually move toward a center or point. This explains why men are often frustrated in communicating with women. Women are apt to expand with a topic while men want them to get to the point.

Generally, when a man speaks, he has already silently mulled over his thoughts until he knows the main idea he wants to communicate. A woman does not necessarily speak to make a point; speaking assists her in discovering her point. By exploring her thoughts and feelings out loud, she discovers where she wants to go.

Just as men need to pull away to mull over an idea, women find greater clarity by expanding and sharing. When a woman begins sharing, she is not always aware of where it will take her, but she trusts that it will take her where she needs to go. For women, sharing is a potent process of self-discovery.

Many times men get frustrated with women simply because they don't understand this difference. They unknowingly interfere with this natural feminine process, or they judge it as a waste of time. A man who understands this difference is able to nurture and support a woman through nonjudgmental listening.

MAY 19

How We Are Different

*O*nce we accept that people are different, we can seriously begin to explore how we are different. Ultimately all human beings are unique, and it is impossible to categorize them. But by creating a greater awareness of our possible differences, the following systems are immensely helpful.

The study of morphology divides people into three body types that are associated with major psychological differences: action oriented, feeling oriented, and mind oriented.

The ancient practice of astrology describes twelve psychological types.

Sufi teachings recognize nine basic psychological types, called the enneagram.

Many contemporary personal growth and business seminars describe the following four types: supporter, promoter, controller, and analyzer. It is proposed that the individual potentially possesses all of these qualities and with a greater awareness can choose to develop and integrate them.

Some oppose categorizing people, since this may limit them or box them in. To say one person is analytical while another is emotional may give rise to judgment. This fear arises because experience tells us that when we are being judged as less than another, it is because we are being categorized in some way; we are being seen as different. Hence we fear being different.

From one perspective, judgments and prejudice are associated with differences. At a deeper level, we can clearly see that the original cause of these judgments is lack of acceptance and appreciation of our differences.

Though the acknowledgment of differences can be perceived as a threat, it is not. By accepting that people are different, we are freed from the compulsion to change them. When we are not preoccupied with changing others, we are free to appreciate their unique values. Ultimately the recognition of differences among people allows us to release our judgments.

The Magic of Doing Little Things

*I*t's magic when a man does little things for a woman. It keeps her love tank full and the score even. When the score is even, or almost even, a woman knows she is loved, which makes her more trusting and loving in return. When a woman knows she's loved, she can love without resentment.

Doing little things for a woman is also healing for a man. In fact, those little things will tend to heal his resentments as well as hers. He begins to feel powerful and effective because as she's getting the caring she needs she can appreciate him in response. Both are then fulfilled.

A man needs to feel he can make a difference, while a woman needs to feel she can depend on him.

Just as a man needs to continue doing little things for a woman, she needs to be particularly attentive to appreciate the little things he does for her. With a smile and a thanks, she can let him know he has scored a point. A man needs this appreciation and encouragement to continue giving. He stops giving when he feels he is being taken for granted. A woman needs to let him know that what he is doing is appreciated.

This doesn't mean that she has to pretend that everything is now perfectly wonderful because he has emptied the trash for her. She can simply notice that he has emptied the trash and say thanks. Gradually more love will flow from both sides.

※※

When Women Aren't Interested in Sex

*M*en feel discouraged when they feel that their wives don't seem to find sex as important as they do. Without consistent, clear messages from her that she enjoys sex, he may lose his attraction to her. Suddenly women he doesn't know, who haven't yet rejected him, become more attractive.

Historically men have been much more sexually active outside marriage than women. Without good communication and romantic skills, couples lose a great degree of their sexual interest in each other.

While women might have sought fulfillment in their fantasies, men have acted theirs out by having affairs.

In the past, women could more easily give up the need for sex in favor of the routine requirement of creating a home and family. The survival of the family was more important than the fulfillment of sexual passions. Sexual fulfillment was a luxury women couldn't afford. Men coped with the lessening of women's sexual interest by discreetly finding sex elsewhere.

Unfortunately, as soon as a man directs his energies elsewhere, it is much harder for his partner to feel sufficiently fulfilled to direct her sexual passions toward him. As a result, the family unit was preserved, but romance was lost.

The major reason men would resort to affairs was that they did not understand that they had the power to reawaken their partner's sexuality. They did not have the skills that we can now apply. With a deeper understanding of the opposite sex, we can now rekindle the flame of passion even when it has blown out.

MAY 22

Finding Balance

*W*hen both sexes are able to balance focused awareness and open awareness, their creativity is enriched. When they are able to balance their work activities with their relationships, greater fulfillment and success is assured. When they can react from their minds as well as their hearts, they can respond to others with love and other positive attitudes.

How can balance be achieved? To find balance, people need to understand, accept, appreciate, and respect both sides of their nature, masculine and feminine. Respecting, loving, and nurturing the feminine in his wife can help a man find balance. In a similar way, a woman's love, trust, and appreciation of the man in her life helps her to find balance.

MAY 23

❧❧

Honor and Respect Lead to Fulfillment

*I*n male/female relationships, the solution is not in denying that differences exist. The potential for conflict is resolved solely by honoring and respecting each other and finding creative ways to fulfill our differing needs.

Each time we take the sometimes painful or difficult step to positive resolution in our personal relationships, we are paving the way for harmony in the world. Your every effort makes it easier for others to follow you.

MAY 24

❧❧

Inner Potential

*W*hile many differences show up in our personalities, our true inner potential to give transcends our sexual differences. Each one of us is meant to be:

1. purposeful
2. intelligent

3. creative
4. loving
5. powerful
6. decisive
7. self-reliant

Each and every one of us has our own unique blend of these essential human qualities. Naturally, every person has limitations, but those limitations are not determined by sex. To assume that gender determines our ability to love, or to express power, or to understand is a great mistake. Such attitudes box people into imaginary categories and inhibit the full expression of who we are and what we can do.

MAY 25

Conventional Relationships

*I*n conventional relationships, the man is more masculine and the woman is more feminine. The attraction lessens over time if the woman repeatedly experiences that she cannot be supported on her female side. Rather than risk the pain of repeated invalidation or rejection, she closes up and becomes in certain ways more masculine.

The same is true for men. Rather than continuing to do masculine things like make decisions, initiate sex, and solve problems for her, when he doesn't feel appreciated he suppresses his male side. In various ways he will automatically become more feminine. Without the sexual polarity, the attraction between partners dissipates.

Although couples may start out very masculine and feminine, over time they begin to reverse roles emotionally. When a man doesn't feel his masculine side being supported, he automatically begins to go out of balance. Likewise, when a woman doesn't get the support she needs at the office and at home to be feminine, she also goes out of balance.

MAY 26

Giving vs. Receiving

*W*omen are very aware of and verbal about the way men change in a relationship, but they are not as aware of the way they change. Women change too. They think that once they are in an exclusive relationship, or engaged, or married, a man will automatically do even more. The woman's expectations increase. In anticipation, she feels inclined to do more for him. Although this may seem like a good idea, it is not.

> *Giving more than she is receiving eventually prevents a woman from appreciating what a man is offering.*

Because she feels she is giving more, she is no longer as excited and appreciative of the little things he does. Instead of growing in appreciation, she begins to take her partner for granted. She begins to expect more from him because she begins to give more: she eagerly begins doing little things for him, she becomes more accommodating, she opens her schedule for him, she makes plans for him, she makes reservations for him, she worries for him, she waits for him, she tries to please him, and so on. By doing more, she stops appreciating the little things he does.

It is fine to give to a man, but learning to receive is better. When a man feels appreciated, he is drawn into a relationship and has more interest and energy to give. A woman lays the foundation for a successful relationship by making a deliberate effort not to give more than she is getting. By being receptive and responsive to what a man offers, she is actually giving the relationship the best chance to grow.

❦

She Needs Devotion, and He Needs Admiration

*W*hen a man gives priority to a woman's needs and proudly commits himself to supporting and fulfilling her, her need to feel cherished is fulfilled. A woman thrives when she feels adored and special. A man fulfills her need to be loved in this way when he makes her feelings and needs more important than his other interests—like work, study, and recreation. When a woman feels she is number one in his life, she admires him.

Just as a woman needs to feel a man's devotion, a man has a primary need to feel a woman's admiration. To admire a man is to regard him with wonder, delight, and pleased approval. A man feels admired when a woman is happily amazed by his unique characteristics or talents, which may include humor, strength, persistence, integrity, honesty, romance, kindness, love, understanding, and other so-called old-fashioned virtues. When a man feels admired, he feels secure enough to devote himself to a woman and adore her.

MAY 28

Unity in Diversity

*A*ccepting our psychological differences frees us to experience an underlying oneness that permeates our relationships. In an abstract way, we are all the same. In every spiritual teaching there is an acknowledgment of that oneness. When our hearts are open, we not only love those close to us, but deep within we feel a spiritual oneness with the world as well. When we read of children suffering from hunger, we feel in our hearts the pain we would feel if they were our own children.

Ultimately we are all motivated to break free from the chains that separate us and to realize our oneness. This opening of the heart is really an awareness that what is outside us is also inside us. The quest to open the heart takes a variety of forms: the path to enlightenment, the quest for God, the dreams of happy marriage, finding one's soul mate, or creating a loving family. In each example, one is inexplicably drawn to something and someone else. By learning to love and be loved, we are satisfying our most basic spiritual purpose in this world.

MAY 29

~~~

Sharing Dark Feelings

*W*hen a woman doesn't feel safe to share her hidden and dark feelings, her only alternative is to avoid intimacy and sex or to suppress and numb her feelings through such addictions as drinking, overeating, overworking, or overcaretaking. Even with her addictions, she will periodically fall into her well, and her feelings may come up in a most uncontrolled fashion.

You probably know stories of couples who never fight or argue, and then suddenly, to everyone's surprise, they decide to get a divorce. In many of these cases, the woman has suppressed her negative feelings to avoid having fights. As a result, she becomes numb and unable to feel her love.

When negative feelings are suppressed, positive feelings are suppressed as well, and love dies. Avoiding arguments and fights certainly is healthy, but not by suppressing feelings. Although it is not necessary to share all your upset or negative feelings, it is important that you take time to hear them yourself. By staying in touch with your feelings, whether you are a man or a woman, not only will you be able to feel the love in your heart but you will also stay young, healthy, creative, sexy, and purposeful.

MAY 30

Making a Difference in the World

*B*y mastering the secrets of passion and practicing forgiveness, we are not only creating a lifetime of love for ourselves but also making a difference in the world.

Practicing new relationship skills and learning to harmonize dissonant values is not only the prerequisite for creating more passionate relationships but directly contributes to a more peaceful world.

Imagine a world where families are not shattered by divorce and neighbors do not hate each other. This kind of world is possible. Each step you take in your relationship helps actualize that possibility. Peace and prosperity for the world become more of a reality each time they approach being your daily reality.

MAY 31

The Need for Balance

*E*very man and every woman has both male and female energies. We could not exist without this combination. The internal imbalance of these complementary forces determines many of the problems we experience in a relationship.

When a man has developed more masculine (contractive) tendencies than feminine (expansive) tendencies, he will appear self-centered and selfish at times, when in truth he is just not focused on the needs of others. He will appear to be uncaring, but his real problem is his inability to tap into his feminine potential, through which he can easily be aware of the needs of others.

Similarly, a woman who has an excess of feminine energy will be overly concerned with others and have little awareness of herself. When experiencing the stress of not getting what she needs, she expands even more. She becomes more responsive to the needs of others but forgets herself. She sacrifices herself without even knowing that she's doing it. At a time when she needs more, she is unable to assert herself or share her wishes because she is unaware of them.

Just as a man under stress appears ungiving or uncaring because he contracts, a woman appears unreceptive or unsupportable because she expands. To avoid these extreme states, men need to explore, develop, and balance both their masculine and feminine sides, and women must do likewise. By blending these complementary energies, not only do our relationships improve but we also become more creative.

❧ JUNE ❧

Investigate, Communicate, Accept

During the month of June, remind yourself that your ability to feel love is directly proportional to your ability to love and accept yourself. Take time to identify any blocks you have to loving. Investigate your heart. Find any corners where you are holding back your love. Make the effort to give again. Let yourself be bigger and forgive those in your past. Let go and move on.

Free yourself from the limits of your past. When we are able to accept, appreciate, and respect others, quite automatically we begin to accept and appreciate ourselves. The more we accept who we are, the more love we will have to share.

Who are you really? What is most important to you? What do you really want in your relationships? These are good questions to ponder. There is a fine line between the healthy desire to improve oneself and forcing undesired change upon oneself or others. The key is to investigate.

Make a deliberate effort to hear your deeper feelings and accept where you are in your soul's journey in this world. Listen deeply to your soul's desire, and know that you are in the right place and at the right time to take your next steps of growth.

Accept the person you are today, recognizing that you deserve to be loved just the way you are. Although we are all in the process of becoming more, we still deserve to be loved and accepted for who we are today. You are good enough to be loved and accepted just the way you are.

JUNE 1

Accepting You

*A*s a result of unsatisfactory relationships, many people today are obsessed with changing themselves, hoping that when they change, their lives will improve. But creating more love in your life has nothing to do with changing who you are or trying to change others. As a matter of fact, that just gets in the way. The more you try to modify your behavior to act as you think you "should" act, the less you will be yourself and the harder it will be for you and others to love you.

There is nothing wrong with wanting to change except when it prevents you from being who you really are. When change is motivated by self-hatred, it can never create more love. You may become more powerful; you may get a better job; you may even make new friends. But you're not going to love yourself more. You may succeed in convincing others that you are worthy of their love, but deep down inside you will never feel truly loved and accepted for just being you. Change and growth are a healthy part of life, but we need to remember that what we are today is already good enough and worthy of love and acceptence.

JUNE 2

Doing Less but Supporting More

*T*he most successful approach in a relationship is to focus first on creating good communication. When a man does not feel blamed or attacked, he is able to feel more empathetic, sympathetic, and understanding. As he begins to listen more, and a woman appreciates him for supporting her in this way, he will almost magically begin to do more of what is most important for her.

To get what she needs from a man, a woman must learn how to communicate needs and desires without demanding or finger-pointing. In most cases, a woman can be made happier by a man who is actually doing less because he is supporting her differently. By doing less, a man can be more supportive. When a man understands this truth, his motivation to do things differently greatly increases.

Part of a man's frustration when a woman wants more is that he mistakenly assumes he has to provide everything she needs. He does not know that as long as he is taking small steps toward helping her around the house and practicing better communication, she will be immeasurably happier.

As both partners begin to give and receive the support they really need, they will happily give increasingly more. He will give her more of what modern women most need and appreciate. She will give him the love and acceptance that he wants.

JUNE 3

The Importance of Communication

*S*ometimes, before a woman can appreciate romantic gestures, she needs to communicate and feel heard. Just as sex connects a man to his feelings, communication connects a woman to her need for and appreciation of romance.

For the last twenty years, the lack of communication in intimate relationships has been the major complaint of women. The reason for this is simple: overworked women need to talk more about their feelings in order to cope successfully with the stress of being overwhelmed.

Learning to fulfill this new need of his partner puts a man back in the saddle. He is able to provide for her in a new and very important way. By gradually learning to listen, a man helps release a woman from feeling overwhelmed and gives her a reason to greatly appreciate him. This frees her to be more responsive in the bedroom.

~~~

How to Communicate Without Blame

A man commonly feels attacked and blamed by a woman's feelings, especially when she is upset and talks about problems. Since he doesn't understand how men and women are different, he doesn't readily relate to her need to talk about all of her feelings.

He mistakenly assumes that she is telling him about her feelings because she thinks he is somehow responsible or to blame. Since she is upset and she is talking to him, he assumes she is upset with him. When she complains, he hears blame. Many men don't understand the Venusian need to share upset feelings with the people they love.

With practice and an awareness of our differences, women can learn how to express their feelings without having them sound like blaming. To reassure a man that he is not being blamed when a woman expresses her feelings, she could pause after a few minutes of sharing and tell him how much she appreciates him for listening.

She could make some of the following comments:

"I'm sure glad I can talk about it."

"It sure feels good to talk about it."

"I'm feeling so relieved that I can talk about this."

"I'm sure glad I can complain about this. It makes me feel so much better."

"Well, now that I've talked about it, I feel much better. Thank you."

This simple change can make a world of difference.

A New Dilemma

*T*he contemporary woman is faced with a new dilemma. Either she trains herself to talk like a man and loses a part of herself as well as an essential source of happiness, or she disregards a man's resistance and lets her feelings fly. In response to her free expression of feelings, he stops listening, and she eventually loses his love and support. Since neither approach works, it's fortunate that there is another way.

Traditionally, women haven't had to depend on men for nurturing conversations, nor have they been required to talk like men throughout the day. If a woman had to be more linear occasionally when she talked with a man, it was okay because she had the whole day to talk in an expanded female style.

The need for women to communicate with men is a new challenge for both. By applying new feminine skills, a woman can greatly assist a man in listening to her feelings. Once a man is prepared, a woman can relax and let go. This is the secret. By saying a few words, a woman can condition a man to deal with her different style of communicating. Even if her words would normally sound critical and blaming to a man in the Martian language, even if he is not yet good at ducking and dodging, if he is prepared correctly, he can even handle a direct hit.

JUNE 6

What Makes Sex Great

*I*deally, for sex to be great there must be loving and supportive communication in the relationship. This is the first step.

When sex gets better, suddenly the whole relationship gets better. Through great sex, the man begins to feel more love, and as a result the woman starts getting the love she may have been missing.

Automatically communication and intimacy increase. A great sex life gives a man the emotional fuel and energy to be attentive and interested in his partner. Men who lose interest are generally not getting their sexual needs satisfied. Not only is sex fun, but it is the doorway to a man's heart. It allows him to open up and feel the tender feelings of love that often become locked up.

JUNE 7

Four Magic Words of Support

*T*he four magic words to support a man are "It's not your fault."

When a woman is expressing her upset feelings, she can support a man by pausing occasionally to encourage him by saying, "I really appreciate your listening, and if this sounds as if I'm saying it's your fault, that is not what I mean. It's not your fault."

A woman can learn to be sensitive to her listener when she understands his tendency to start feeling like a failure when he hears a lot of problems. Reassuring a man that it is not his fault or that he is not being blamed works only as long as she truly is not blaming him or criticizing him, however.

If she is attacking him, then she should share her feelings with someone else. She should wait until she is more loving and centered to talk to him. She could share her resentful feelings with someone she is not upset with, who will be able to give her the support she needs, or write out her feelings in a private journal. Then when she feels more loving and forgiving, she can successfully approach him to share her feelings.

JUNE 8

Expressing Your Negative Emotions

The complete truth about how you are feeling has many levels:

anger
sadness
fear
sorrow
love, understanding, forgiveness, and desire

Normally you are only aware of one emotion at a time, but the rest are all there as well. If all these emotions can be fully experienced and expressed, emotional upsets can be easily resolved. Each emotion must be fully experienced and expressed for the successful completion of the process—if not, the feelings around any upset will never be fully resolved and will most likely be repressed inside you, creating more emotional baggage for you to carry around from relationship to relationship.

By fully expressing all of the negative emotions, you can spontaneously experience your love and understanding again.

Most communication problems stem from communicating only part of the truth, from not expressing the complete truth. Often when people tell the truth, they leave out many of the feelings they are having and focus on one of the above levels, excluding the others. Underneath all negative emotions are positive emotions—underneath all anger and hurt is a feeling of love and a willingness to connect and be close. The people who make you the most angry are the people you care about the most. The problem arises when you communicate anger or hurt and neglect to express the complete truth about the love underneath. By taking time to explore the deeper levels of our upset feelings, we can always come back to feeling an open heart full of love.

~~~

The Prime Objective: Listen

*E*ven if a man is practicing new relationship skills and listening without trying to solve a woman's problems, her questioning can catch him off guard. Besides the fact that men generally don't like too many questions, he is giving answers instead of asking more questions. Instead of listening, he is talking.

The more a man says, the more there is for a woman to question, and the more annoyed he may become. Not only is he uncomfortable but also she is not getting to share her thoughts and feelings. As a simple rule, a man should practice not saying more than a woman and, whenever possible, should delay answering her questions by asking her more questions.

> **The more words she speaks, the more heard
> she can feel and the more appreciated he will be.**

When a woman is bothered about something, a man is tempted to defend his point of view. He instinctively feels that if he could only share his understanding of the situation, she would feel better. In truth, she will feel better only when he shares in her understanding of a situation. When a woman feels understood and validated, she can relax. Otherwise, she feels she has to fight to be heard.

JUNE 10

The Male Need to Be Accepted

*W*hen a man is accepted by a woman, he is received willingly. This attitude cultivates a man's belief in his abilities. When a man's actions are unconditionally accepted, then he feels free to explore ways he can improve. For this reason, acceptance is the basis of behavioral changes in a relationship.

The need for acceptance is especially important for men. Sometimes a woman will accept a man based upon his potential. This is not true acceptance. She is waiting for the day when he will change, and then she will be able to accept him. Men need to be accepted for who they are today, not who they will be tomorrow. A man will tend to become stubborn and resistant to change if he senses that he is not being accepted. Loving a man the way he is nurtures him to become all that he can be.

The Essential Key: Telling the Complete Truth

*C*ommunicating the complete truth about your feelings is essential. It is the first step in resolving emotional tension and enriching your relationships with others. Before you can communicate the truth about what you feel, you have to know what you are feeling in the first place. Once you know the complete truth about how you feel, you are more capable of communicating it in a loving and considerate manner and at the appropriate time and place.

Your ability to feel love is directly proportional to your ability to tell the complete truth. The more truth you have in your life, the more love you will experience. Honest relationships with direct and effective communication are a source of increasing love and self-esteem.

Many times we seek out relationships in order to protect ourselves from the truth. We have a sign up saying: "If you don't tell me the truth, then I won't tell you the truth." These relationships can be easy and comfortable but do not serve to increase your self-love and self-worth.

JUNE 12

❧❧❧

Romance and Communication

*F*or romance to thrive, a woman needs to feel heard and understood on a day-to-day basis. In the beginning of a relationship, the woman really doesn't know the man and can imagine that she is truly seen, understood, and validated. This positive feeling is the fertile ground of romance and passion. After several disappointments, this magic spell is broken.

When the man is untrained in the skills of listening to and understanding a woman, or when the woman resists sharing the feelings that naturally come up, she eventually feels unheard and is turned off. She generally doesn't even know what happened. He may make romantic overtures, but they don't have the same magical feeling. Even cut flowers lose their potency if a woman doesn't feel heard on a daily basis.

Talking is a major feminine need. Creating romantic rituals that say "I love you and I care about you" can go a long way to communicate love without words. With the support of romance, communication is much easier.

How to Listen Without Blaming Back

A man often blames a woman for being blaming when she is innocently talking about problems. This is very destructive to the relationship because it blocks communication.

Imagine a woman saying, "All we ever do is work, work, work. We don't have any fun anymore. You are so serious." A man could very easily feel she is blaming him.

If he feels blamed, I suggest he not blame back by saying, "I feel as if you are blaming me."

Instead, I suggest saying, "It is difficult to hear you say I am so serious. Are you saying it's all my fault that we don't have more fun?"

Or he could say, "It doesn't feel good to me when I hear you say I am so serious and we don't have any fun. Are you saying that it's all my fault?"

In addition, to improve the communication, he can give her a way out through a reality check. He could say, "It feels as if you're saying it's all my fault that we work so much. Is that true?"

Or he could say, "When you say we don't have any fun and that I'm so serious, I feel that you're saying it's all my fault. Are you?"

All of these responses are respectful and give her a chance to take back any blame that he might have felt. When she says, "Oh no,

I'm not saying it's all your fault," he will probably feel somewhat relieved.

Another approach that I find most helpful is to remember that she always has a right to be upset. Once she gets it out, she will not only feel much better but will appreciate him for listening. This awareness allows a man to relax and remember that if he can listen without taking it personally, she will be able to let go of her negative feelings when she needs to complain. Even if she were blaming him, she would not hold onto it.

JUNE 14

Breaking the Language Barrier

*M*ost couples today are not fluent in each other's language. When they talk, they experience increasing frustration instead of fulfillment.

When we consider the new stresses on relationships and family life and the absence of traditional support systems, it is no wonder that it's so hard to stay together, and it explains why millions choose to be single. Neither sex is being nurtured and supported in the ways that matter most, because they are speaking different languages.

It no longer has to be that way. For instance, male frustration could be helped if, at the end of an emotional talk, women could say any combination of the following:

"Thanks so much for listening."

"I just needed to get that out."

"I'm sorry it was difficult for you to hear."

"You can forget everything I just said."

"It doesn't matter as much now."

"I feel much better."

"Thanks for helping me sort this out and letting me talk."

"This conversation has really helped me get a better perspective on things."

"I feel so much better now, thanks for listening."

"Wow, I sure had a lot to say. I feel so much better."

"I feel so much better. Sometimes I just need to talk about things and then my mood changes."

"I appreciate your patience in helping me to sort things out through talking."

Any of these comments would be heaven to a man and would make him feel warmly appreciated. This is because in Martian, his native language, these comments have a special and positive significance.

~≈≈~

Polarity Sex

*T*here are two sexual polarities: giving pleasure and receiving pleasure. When one partner is giving and the other partner is receiving, the sexual pleasure can easily build. In polarity sex, partners take turns consciously using these polarities to increase desire and pleasure. One partner gives while the other receives. Then, later on, they switch, and the giver stops giving and just receives.

Polarity sex has two stages. In the first stage, the man takes and the woman gives. Then, in the second stage, he attends to her needs while she relaxes and focuses on receiving.

While practicing the first stage of polarity sex, the man starts out receiving. He is not primarily concerned with spending a lot of time providing the woman with pleasure. Certainly he wants her to enjoy it, but he is really focused on his own pleasure. Likewise, she is not expecting herself to get turned on right away and keep up with him.

In the second stage, it is her turn to receive while he focuses on giving. She has done all her giving, and now she can just receive. In this way, both people eventually get everything they want.

~~~~~

Giving Men the Right Message

*W*hen a woman expresses the best of her feminine side by being self-assured, receptive, and responsive, it brings out the best of a man's masculine side. The more a man senses that a woman needs what he has to offer, the more interested he becomes. Quite automatically he feels more confident, purposeful, and responsible.

A woman's receptivity attracts and empowers a man.

He is confident because her self-assurance sends a message that there is a job opening. He is purposeful because her receptive smile sends the message that he could get the job to make her happy. She has a need and he has the solution. Her responsiveness encourages him to feel he could be successful in fulfilling her needs. This encouragement makes him feel more responsible to fulfill her needs.

New Communication Skills

To ensure the best communication in a relationship, men and women can begin applying new skills. An easy way for women to remember what is required of them is to remember the four P's: pausing, preparing, postponing, and persisting. In a similar way, men can remember the four D's: ducking, dodging, disarming, and delivering. A relationship will be easiest when both are doing their best. Without these insights, relationships are much more difficult than they need to be.

Instead of simply sharing her feelings, a wise woman will first pause and prepare a man for what he is about to hear. If she has a request to make, she should postpone it until they are feeling mutually positive and supportive. If he forgets to fulfill her requests, she must persist without demanding.

> *These four P's—pausing, preparing, postponing, and persisting—are essential skills for communicating with a Martian.*

To be successful in communicating with a woman, instead of listening passively a man needs to focus his attention on trying to be supportive and avoid being combative. Ducking means not offering solutions to her problems. Dodging means not taking her complaints personally. Trying to understand with genuine sympathy allows him to disarm any blame she may be feeling. Waiting to comment and then giving a supportive statement of compassion, understanding, or assistance allows him to deliver his support successfully.

> *The four D's—ducking, dodging, disarming, and delivering—are essential in listening to a Venusian.*

One of the biggest obstacles to practicing these four skills for both women and men is not understanding that men and women essentially speak different languages. A man could be growing in his skills slowly but surely, but when he fails to listen or respect a woman's feelings, she may feel it is hopeless. In a similar way, a woman may be progressing in supporting her male partner, but when she forgets to pause and prepare and he feels blamed, he may automatically assume that nothing is working.

By understanding the different languages we speak, it is much easier to recognize that our partners do love us and that they are doing their best, in their own way. It takes time to change old habits and learn new ones, but with persistence and loving patience, communication will become much easier.

JUNE 18

The Need to Change Him

*T*o a man, real love is when you don't try to change a person. When a man meets the right woman, he will let his heart come out and love this woman just as she is. A man wants the same in return, but most women don't know that.

When a woman is shopping for her partner, she looks for a man who makes her feel good, whom she cares for and loves. Somewhere there's a feeling welling up inside, "He's got potential; I see it. What I could do with him. Love will overcome. I'll just love him. I'll just give to him and he will change."

Unfortunately, men, there's nothing you can do to change that about women. That's the way they are. But women can learn to work with that, just as men can learn to accept that at times a woman is just going to want to change them. When a woman persists in appreciating a man, it helps to compensate for the times he feels she wants to change him.

❧⟶

When to Talk with a Man

*W*hen a man is pulling away, it is not the time to talk or try to get closer. Let him pull away. After some time, he will return. He will appear loving and supportive and will act as though nothing has happened. This is the time to talk.

When a woman wants to talk or feels the need to get close, she should do the talking and not expect a man to initiate the conversation. To initiate a conversation, she needs to be the first to begin sharing, even if her partner has little to say.

***As a woman appreciates a man for listening,
gradually he will have more to say.***

A man can be very open to having a conversation with a woman but at first have nothing to say. What women don't know about Martians is that they need to have a reason to talk. They don't talk just for the sake of sharing. When a woman talks for a while, a man will start to open up and talk about how he relates to what she has said.

For example, if she talks about some of her difficulties during the day, he may share some of the difficulties of his day so that they can understand each other. If she talks about her feelings about the kids, he may then talk about his feelings about the kids. If he doesn't feel blamed or pressured as she opens up, then he gradually begins to open up.

JUNE 20

~≈~

Good Communication

*I*f a woman doesn't feel safe in talking about her feelings, she will eventually have nothing to say. Creating the safety for her to talk freely without having to fear rejection, interruption, or ridicule allows a woman to thrive in a relationship. Over time, she can continue to trust and love her partner more if he is a good listener.

Men quite commonly grow bored when women tell them the details of their days. They are more interested in the bottom line. As a man begins to understand how much a woman appreciates and benefits from his full attention, then listening and sharing stops being a chore and becomes an important nurturing ritual. With open lines of communication, a woman will continue to grow.

JUNE 21

~≈~

It's Okay to Make Mistakes

*N*o one is perfect and no partner is perfect. One of the greatest gifts of love is to accept our partner's limitations as well as our own. The seed of love cannot grow unless it is planted in the fertile ground of forgiveness. To thrive in a relationship we need to remember again and again that it is okay to make mistakes. Through forgiving mistakes and accepting life's imperfection we are actually exercising and thus strengthening our ability to love and be loved.

JUNE 22

The Summer of Love

*T*hroughout the summer of our love, we realize that our partner is not as perfect as we thought and that we have to work on our relationship. Our partner is not only from another planet but is also a human being who makes mistakes and is flawed in certain ways.

Frustration and disappointment arise. Weeds need to be uprooted, and plants need extra watering under the hot sun. It is no longer easy to give love and get the love we need. We discover that we are not always happy, and we do not always feel loving. It is not our picture of love.

Many couples become disillusioned at this point. They do not want to work on a relationship. They unrealistically expect it to be spring all the time. They blame their partners and give up. They do not realize that love is not always easy; sometimes it requires hard work under a hot sun. In the summer season of love, we need to nurture our partner's needs as well as to ask for the love we need. It doesn't happen automatically. With patience, skill, and persistence, the flowers of love will grow and blossom.

How to Get a Man to Listen

*W*hen a woman says, "You don't understand," she really means, "You don't understand that right now I don't need a solution."

He hears that she doesn't appreciate his solution and then gets hooked into arguing about the validity of his approach and explaining himself at a time when she only needs to talk.

Here's an alternative for the woman. First pause and consider that he is doing his best to understand, and then say, "Let me try saying that a different way."

When a man hears this phrase, it conveys the message that he has not fully understood her but in a noncritical way. He is much more willing to listen and reconsider what she is saying. He does not feel criticized or blamed and as a result is more eager to support her. Without understanding what makes men tick, it would be nearly impossible for a woman to figure out that a man would greatly prefer to hear "Let me try saying this a different way" to "You don't understand." To a man, the difference is so obvious that he would never think to suggest it.

JUNE 24

Communication and Motivation

*T*o get what they need from their men, women must learn how to communicate needs and desires without demanding or finger-pointing. In most cases, as we will discover, a woman can be made happier by a man who is actually doing less but focusing his energies on being a better communicator. As a man understands her experience of life better and feels appreciated for listening, his motivation to do things differently greatly increases.

JUNE 25

It's Not What We Say but the Way That We Say It

*W*omen unknowingly start and escalate arguments first by sharing negative feelings about their partner's behavior and then by giving unsolicited advice. When a woman neglects to buffer her negative feelings with messages of trust and acceptance, a man responds negatively, leaving the woman confused.

*Most women are unaware of
how painful their mistrust is to a man.*

To avoid painful arguments, we need to remember that our partner objects not to what we are saying but to how we are saying it. It takes two to argue, but it only takes one to stop an argument. The best way to stop an argument is to nip it in the bud. Take responsibility for recognizing when a disagreement is turning into a painful argument. Stop talking and take a time-out.

During your time-out, reflect on how you were approaching your partner. Try to understand in what way you were not giving him what he needs. After some time has passed, come back and talk again but in a loving and respectful way. Time-outs allow us to cool off, heal our wounds, and center ourselves before trying to communicate again.

JUNE 26

Asking for What You Want

Some people resent having to ask for what they want in a relationship. They feel, "If my partner really loves me, he will know what to do." Don't expect your partner to know what's inside you or to read your mind. Tell your partner what you want, and don't forget to ask what they want from you too.

If you aren't getting what you want, start letting your partner know in advance and not just after the letdown. Keeping what you want a secret is a sure way to build up feelings of resentment and hurt between you and your partner.

You and your partner can't always have everything you want in your relationship, but if you are compatible, you can work it out so that both of you can be satisfied. Ask for what you want and be willing to negotiate so that both of you get your needs met. In this way, you and your partner both win and no one loses.

JUNE 27

She Needs Understanding, and He Needs Acceptance

*W*hen a man listens without judgment but with empathy and relatedness as a woman expresses her feelings, she feels heard and understood. An understanding attitude doesn't presume to know a person's thoughts or feelings. Instead it gathers meaning from what is heard and moves toward validating what is being communicated.

The more a woman's need to be heard and understood is fulfilled, the easier it is for her to give a man the acceptance he needs.

When a woman lovingly receives a man without trying to change him, he feels accepted. An accepting attitude does not reject but affirms that he is being favorably received. It does not mean the woman believes he is perfect but indicates that she is not trying to improve him, that she trusts him to make his own improvements. When a man feels accepted, it is much easier for him to listen and to give her the understanding she needs and deserves.

JUNE 28

A Woman's Lifeline

Good communication is a modern woman's lifeline. Without it, she loses touch with her ability to feel the love in her heart and to receive the loving support of others; she loses her ability to feel warm, tender, and sweet feelings. By learning to support a man in a particular way, she can ensure getting back the support she needs to nurture her female side.

To achieve this end, it is important for her to realize that men have never been required to be good listeners to a woman's feelings and that they don't know how. Clearly understanding this fact will give her the patience and the awareness to appreciate each step he makes toward her fulfillment.

> **Men have never been required to be good listeners:**
> **it is a new skill, and it takes time to learn.**

Women generally believe that if a man loves them, he will want to listen to their feelings. A man doesn't feel this way, because sharing feelings is not as important to him, and traditionally women didn't want to share their feelings with men.

It actually works the other way around. The more a man cares, the more it hurts when he gets hit, if he hasn't learned how to duck and dodge. When she is unhappy, it is much harder for him to listen without feeling blamed. It is harder because the more he loves her, the more he feels like a failure when she is not feeling loved and supported.

By understanding that a man really needs her support to support her successfully, a woman can be motivated to help him without feeling as if she is begging for love. The insight that a man can care deeply but also resist her when she starts sharing feelings helps her to take responsibility for communicating in ways that are supportive for herself and for him as well.

Time Alone

When you are living alone in your own separate world, it is very easy to continue repressing or numbing your uncomfortable or painful feelings. This is why some people avoid relationships. It would take too much effort and energy for them to continue repressing their feelings around another person.

Some people can only stand relationships for a certain amount of time and then they leave, either physically or emotionally, by shutting down their feelings altogether. You know you are resisting dealing with some repressed feelings when you leave your partner and feel relief.

> **When we need to get away, it is the perfect time**
> **to explore our inner feelings and release**
> **any negativity.**

This is why so many people cry for space in relationships. They walk around with all these repressed emotions and are successful at holding them down until they come home at the end of the day and see each other. As soon as they start to open up, all the unexpressed feelings of the day begin to surface. Rather than deal with them, it is simpler just to stay shut down.

This is not to undermine the need to be alone at times. We all need time alone and time away from any relationship to stay in touch with who we are. The need for autonomy is as important as the need to share. But it should not be used as an excuse to hide one's feelings.

JUNE 30

Spinning Out and Spacing Out

Since we are not perfectly in balance at all times, it is realistic to expect men to space out occasionally while mulling things over, just as it is perfectly normal for women to spin out occasionally while sharing their feelings. This understanding is important because it helps women to be more tolerant of men when they space out and forget things. It also helps men to realize that women are not crazy when they spin out and become overwhelmed.

❧ JULY ❧

Instinct, Imagination, Initiative

A successful relationship depends on your desire to take the initiative. By doing so, you can create new and exciting opportunities for the two of you to rediscover each other.

This month (and every month) use one of the simplest and most powerful ways to rekindle the passion in a relationship: go on a romantic getaway.

Indulge at a bed-and-breakfast inn or a lovely hotel; discover a cabin in the woods, or pitch a lakeside tent for two. Let your imagination run free. Whatever your choice may be, create a special occasion to rekindle the love you have for each other.

Given the right setting, more often than not you will find that your instincts will take you where you truly want to go with your life—and your love.

~~~~~~

When a Man Moves Faster

A woman needs to trust that she can get what she needs in a relationship. She is not easily impressed by a man's strong feelings and promises. On Venus, they tend instinctively to know that feelings are always changing. She needs assurance that his feelings will not change as they get to know each other.

Taking the time to react and behave appropriately for each stage of the relationship will ensure that a man can nurture in a woman the trust she needs to feel before moving to the next stage. When making up after an argument, a man is often quick to assume that everything is fine. He generally needs to give a woman a little more time to fully open up.

Why Men Argue with Feelings

*M*en mistakenly assume that an emotional woman is inflexible in her thinking. They don't realize that when a woman talks about her feelings, she is not drawing conclusions or expressing fixed opinions.

She talks to discover the range of feelings within herself—not to give an accurate description of objective reality. That's what men do. She is more concerned with discovering and describing what is going on in her subjective inner world.

When a woman has a chance to share her feelings freely, she begins to feel more loving. Sometimes she may later realize how wrong, incorrect, or unfair her statements sounded, but in most cases she just forgets them as she begins to see from a more loving perspective.

It's hard for men to relate readily to this mood change because it's foreign to their natures, and they just can't fathom it. When a man is upset and talks with the person who is upsetting him, he tends to remain upset unless that person agrees with him in some significant way or until he can find a solution. Simply listening to him and nodding your head in sympathy is not enough if he is really upset.

After a woman shares a negative feeling, a man mistakenly takes it as her final conclusion and thinks she is blaming him. He doesn't know that her feelings will change if he just lets her talk them out.

JULY 3

~~~~

When Women Give Points

*W*omen possess a special ability to appreciate the little things of life as much as the big things. This is a blessing for men. Most men strive for greater and greater success because they believe it will make them worthy of love. Deep inside, they crave love and admiration from others. They do not know that they can draw that love and admiration to them without having to be a greater success.

A woman has the ability to heal a man of this addiction to success by appreciating the little things he does. As men begin to feel loved for the little things, the pressures to be more and do more that all men feel (or unknowingly feel) are released.

JULY 4

~~~~

The True Meaning of Equality

*M*en and women are created equal; ultimately the essence or spirit of men and women is the same. All men and women have intelligence and loving hearts, but the way we develop and express our individual potential is different for each person.

Our greatest power is to love and support each other. Every person is unique and has a special gift to offer. It is unfortunate that we assume that in order to find equality, we must be the same as others. By respecting and appreciating our singular differences, we give ourselves a chance to blossom and discover our true gifts. In reality, we're all different and interdependent. By recognizing this interdependency, we can learn to express our full power.

JULY 5

The Therapy of Great Sex

*A*ny resentments building up in a man are easily washed away when he experiences great sex. There is no therapy better for a man than great sex. Sometimes therapy or counseling is needed to get to that place where a man and woman can experience great sex, but once a couple is there, great sex keeps a man going and keeps the magic of passionate love alive.

Without the regular experience of great sex, it is very easy for a man to forget how much he loves his partner. He may wish her well and be congenial or civil in the relationship, but he will not feel the deep connection that they felt in the beginning.

Without great sex, her little imperfections will begin to get bigger and bigger in his eyes. Unlike a woman, who needs to talk about feelings to be more loving, a man can feel more loving through great sex.

Although good communication is essential in a relationship and will lead to great sex, when the woman in a relationship doesn't experience great sex over time, she can easily harden under the weight of all her responsibilities. She feels responsible not only for herself but also for her partner. She forgets her own sensual and sexual feminine desires. Without the romantic support of her loving companion, she doesn't feel she has time for herself.

JULY 6

Mirror, Mirror on the Wall

*T*rying to change your partner's emotions or talk them out of a feeling is a sure sign that they are mirroring an emotion you don't want to feel in yourself. You will resist in your partner what you suppress in yourself.

If you are resisting your partner's emotions, you are probably resisting those same emotions within yourself.

If you notice your partner, parent, child, or friend expressing some emotion—anger, fear, sadness, or neediness—and you begin to feel annoyed, irritated, or resistant to them, they are probably expressing some of what you are suppressing inside. Since you resist your emotion, you will resist your partner's similar emotion.

On the other hand, if your partner expresses a feeling and you don't feel annoyed or irritated and can easily comfort them, you are probably not suppressing that emotion. With this insight, you can use your resistance to assist you in discovering and then healing your own suppressed feelings.

JULY 7

Discovering Our Different Emotional Needs

*M*en and women are generally unaware that they have different emotional needs. As a result, they do not instinctively know how to support each other. Men typically give in relationships what men want, while women give what women want. As a result they both end up dissatisfied and resentful.

Men and women feel they give and give but do not get back. They feel their love is unacknowledged and unappreciated. The truth is that they are both giving love but not in the desired manner.

Men and women mistakenly assume that the other sex has the same needs and desires.

For example, a woman thinks she is being loving when she asks a lot of caring questions or expresses concern. This can be very annoying to a man. He may start to feel controlled and want space. This confuses her because if she were offered this kind of support, she would be appreciative.

Similarly, men think they are being loving, but the way they express their love may make a woman feel invalidated and unsupported. For example, when a woman gets upset, he may think he is loving and supporting her by making comments that minimize the importance of her problems. He may say, "Don't worry, it's not such a big deal." Or he may completely ignore her, assuming he is giving her a lot of space to cool off and go into her cave. What he thinks is support makes her feel minimized, unloved, and ignored, because when a woman is upset, she needs to be heard and understood.

Without this insight into different male and female needs, we don't understand why our attempts to help fail.

Mental Attraction for Men

*B*y exercising his discernment and choosing to date only women he is attracted to physically and emotionally, a man begins to develop mental attraction. He is intrigued by a woman and wants to touch not just her body but who she is. He is not just attracted to her physically, nor does he just enjoy being friends with her. He is fascinated by the way she thinks, the way she feels, and the way she conducts her life.

As a man's discernment in partners grows, many women are interesting to him but only a few are outstanding. Only a few women will have the aspects of character to which he is most attracted. He will most successfully increase his discernment by getting to know and getting involved with only these women. Simply feeling physically attracted or friendly is no longer the primary requirement. Now a woman must also be very interesting to him.

In a marriage, a man can increase his mental attraction on a romantic getaway by holding back from having sex right away. Sharing more time in conversation while he is aroused can increase his ability to be interested in his partner and the way she thinks about things. This can also be achieved by making love in the daytime and then talking afterward.

How She Unknowingly Turns Him Off

*W*hen a man fails, he needs time to mull things over and gradually assume responsibility for his mistake. Unfortunately, at such times a woman often has a compulsion to say something like "I told you so" or "You should have . . ." or "You know that . . ." or "How could you . . ." or "Why didn't you . . ." or "You never . . ." or "I know you must feel bad" (I feel so sorry for you).

She mistakenly assumes that these kinds of comments will get him to realize and remember his mistake. Their actual effect is to stimulate his defensiveness, self-righteousness, and forgetfulness. Even if he acknowledges his mistake, he will forget the lesson he should have learned. A man remembers and learns from his mistakes when he is not corrected or rejected for them. He needs the support to correct himself.

What makes the above statements ineffective is that they are all attempts to help him feel or perform better when he hasn't asked for help. One of the most valuable things a person can say to a man under stress is "What happened?" This helps him to center himself by becoming more objective.

Initiating Sex vs. Conversation

*W*hen a man is confident of his partner's positive feelings about sex, he will generally keep initiating sex. If he feels that he is repeatedly rejected or that he has to convince her to have sex, he will stop initiating. Eventually he will become sexually passive and less interested.

For a man to grow in passion, he needs to feel free to initiate sex. Just as a woman needs to feel that her partner will listen to her feelings in a positive way without rejecting her, a man needs to feel he can initiate sex without being rejected.

When a man is not in the mood for conversation, he needs to say so gracefully. He can say, "I want to understand your feelings, but first I need some time alone, and then we can talk." When a man works to show he is interested in his partner's feelings and cares enough to come back and initiate conversation, she feels loved.

In a similar way, when a woman is not in the mood for sex but is careful to let a man know that she loves sex with him, he feels loved. When a woman is not in the mood, a man needs to hear that soon she will be back, ready and happy to have sex with him.

With this awareness, a woman automatically becomes more responsive to his sensitivity and is more motivated to find ways for him to feel free to initiate sex. Just as great communication opens a woman up to enjoy great sex, the possibility of great sex directly helps a man to be more loving in a relationship.

The Need for Clear Signals

A woman needs clear communication signals to know when a man is open and when he is closed, in the same way that a man needs to know when she is open to solutions and when she just needs to be heard.

Just as it is hard for a man to trust that a woman will feel better again after sharing negative feelings, it is equally difficult for a woman to trust that a man loves her when he pulls away and ignores her.

A woman needs to pause before talking or making requests of a man, to find out if he is in the cave. If he is not available, she has to postpone getting her needs met by him. If she can support him in this way, not only will he spend less time in the cave, he will be much more loving when he is out of the cave.

By persisting in this process of not trying to change him but instead helping to make him successful in supporting her, a woman can dramatically improve her relationship.

When a man is in his cave, it is the time for a woman to be less demanding of him. This nondemanding and trusting attitude is very attractive to a man and will definitely shorten cave time.

※

Why He Wants a Relationship

*M*en and women come to relationships for different reasons. A man is most interested in a relationship when he feels he has something to offer and share. When he feels good about himself and his work, he wants to share that with a woman. The more competent a man feels in the presence of a woman, the more attracted he will be to her.

To increase the opportunity for a man to feel attracted to a her, a woman might ask his advice on something. Whenever a man gets to feel useful to a woman, he will feel more proud of himself and like her more. The more interested a woman is in what a man can offer her, the more interested he becomes in her.

When she does ask for his advice, her response is very important. If she disagrees with his advice or doesn't like it, she must be careful to allow him to save face. He needs at least to get the message that she appreciated his attempt to help. Another man would instinctively know how to do this, but a woman will not.

These are the kind of comments any man would give to another out of respect:

"That's a good idea. I would never have thought of that. Thanks. That's very helpful."

"That's a great point. It really helps me finally figure out what to do."

"That makes sense. I'm glad I talked to you. Hearing different points of view sure helps to clarify things. Thanks."

JULY 13

A Man with a Slow Hand

*H*aving a great sex life doesn't mean you experience fireworks every time, but it does require you to persist in being aware of your partner's different needs. Ideally, each time they make love, both the man and the woman should feel they are getting what they need.

A man commonly tends to forget what a woman needs to be fulfilled in sex. In the beginning, he may go very slowly in sex because he is not sure of what she likes or he is not sure that she is willing to let him touch her. Once they are having sex regularly, he speeds up. He doesn't realize that it was his slow and tentative movements that were so arousing to her. Even when a man has read about these differences, he may easily forget them in the heat of his passion because they are not his instinctive experience.

Mental Monogamy

*N*ot only are men not taught why monogamy is important, they are not taught how to be monogamous. The technique is very simple. When a man notices another woman and starts getting turned on, he should just begin thinking about having sex with his wife or recall a particularly exciting memory of having sex with his wife.

This way, each time he gets turned on, his sexual energy is consciously directed to his partner. After five to eight years of this practice, he will become even more attracted to his wife. He will also have learned to master his sexual energy. Not only will his wife grow in passion with him, but he will have more power and success in his life.

Psychological Differences Between Men and Women

*M*en and women are not only biologically and anatomically different, they are psychologically different as well. For example, it is universally observed that compared with men, women are more intuitive, are more interested in love and relationships, and experience different reactions to stress. They also have different kinds of complaints and problems in relationships. To suggest, as many have, that these differences are entirely cultural and conditioned into us from childhood is absurd.

Certainly cultural and parental conditioning affect how the sexes differ, but they are not responsible for our primary differences. From a pragmatic point of view, these are determined physically by differences in our DNA programming. As children grow, they are further influenced by family and cultural conditioning.

It is impossible to give a particular stereotyped image that works for every man or for every woman. In general, we can safely say that to nurture and value oneself while pursuing the development of one's potential is the answer to this continuing quest. Giving up one's primary qualities and characteristics in favor of another's is not.

JULY 16

Opening the Car Door

*R*omantic rituals or habits are ways the truth of your deepest feelings can be easily expressed. Opening the car door is one of those rituals. Particularly for men, doing such things is a way of showing love. When a woman appreciates his efforts, not only does he feel closer to her, but also her heart begins to open as well.

When a couple goes out on a date, he should go to her side of the car and open the door—even if the car automatically unlocks with a little beeper. If he starts forgetting to do this, she can remind him the next time as they approach the car by simply wrapping her arm inside his so that he naturally escorts her to the door.

Even if he is opening the door for her, the very feminine act of cuddling next to her man and wrapping her arm around him is very nurturing both for her and for him.

~~~~

Silencing Your Feelings through Addictions

*C*ertainly you've had the experience of feeling gripped by negative emotions. As adults we generally try to control these negative emotions by avoiding them. Our addictions can be used to silence the painful cries of our feelings and unfulfilled needs. After a glass of wine, the pain is gone for a moment, but it will come back again and again. Ironically, the very act of avoiding our negative emotions gives them the power to control our lives.

> **By learning to listen to and nurture our inner emotions,
> we gradually loosen their grip.**

Our unresolved childhood emotions have the power to control us by gripping our adult awareness and preventing loving communication. Until we are able to listen lovingly to these seemingly irrational feelings from our past, which seem to intrude into our life when we most need our sanity, they will continue to obstruct loving communication.

The secret of communicating our difficult feelings lies in first taking the time to write out our negative feelings until we get to the positive feelings underneath. The more we are able to communicate to our partners with the love they deserve, the better our relationships will be. When you are able to share your upset feelings in a loving way, it becomes much easier for your partner to hear and support you in return.

When a Man Can Control His Passion

*W*hen a man can feel his passion and control it, a woman can begin to let go of control, release her inhibitions, and feel her passions. As a man learns to control his passions, not only does he help his partner reach higher levels of fulfillment, but he also can experience greater levels of sexual pleasure and love.

When a man is in control, it means that his passion is so great that he could easily have an orgasm, but instead he holds back and gradually builds up his partner's passion. When a man is unable to keep control in sex, he can easily find this control through releasing his sexual energy in the shower the day before. When the pressure to have an orgasm is released the day before, then automatically he will have more control.

Another way to increase staying power is to practice exercising his PC muscles. To locate the PC, practice restricting the flow while urinating. The muscles required to do this are the PC. After you have identified them, exercise them each day by contracting ten times three times a day. As these muscles strengthen, stronger sexual control becomes much easier and then automatic.

JULY 19

Mental Chemistry for Men

*C*ontinuing to exercise his growing discernment by choosing to date only women who attract him on all three levels—physical, emotional, and mental—a man begins to realize his ability to feel soul attraction.

> **Having all three levels of attraction opens the door to experiencing a soul attraction.**

His love recognizes that this person, though imperfect, is perfect for him. His love allows him to see the good in his partner and motivates him to be supportive. As his love grows, he is able to discern whether this is the right person for him. This decision is not based on a list of conditions. The mind doesn't figure it out. The soul just knows.

JULY 20

Healing Negative Feelings

*U*nderstanding and accepting another's negative feelings is difficult if your own negative feelings have not been heard or supported.

The more we are able to heal our own unresolved feelings from childhood, the easier it is to share our feelings and to listen to our partner's feelings without being hurt, impatient, frustrated, or offended.

The more resistance you have to feeling your inner pain, the more resistance you will have to listening to the feelings of others. If you feel impatient and intolerant when others express their childlike feelings, this is an indicator of how you treat yourself.

> *To heal our hearts,*
> *we must reparent ourselves.*

We must acknowledge that there is an emotional person inside us who gets upset even when our rational adult mind says there is no reason to be upset. We must isolate that emotional part of ourself and become a loving parent to it. We need to ask ourselves: "What's the matter? Are you hurt? What are you feeling? What happened to upset you? What are you angry about? What makes you sad? What are you afraid of? What do you want?"

When we listen to our feelings with compassion, our negative feelings quite miraculously are healed, and we are able to respond to situations in a much more loving and respectful way. By understanding our childlike feelings, we automatically open a door for loving feelings to permeate what we say.

When Men Stop Initiating Sex

*O*ne of the major reasons a couple stops having sex is that a man stops initiating sex, or a woman initiates sex too much. When a woman does all the initiating, not only does she gradually become frustrated, but after a while a man will begin to lose interest in sex with her.

Women generally do not understand that if they pursue a man more than he pursues them, the man will eventually become more passive. A little pursuing energy is fine to let him know when it is a good time for him to pursue her, but when she does it all, he loses interest and doesn't even know why.

When a woman initiates sex all the time,
a man may become more passive and lose interest.

When a woman feels too responsible for initiating sex, a man slowly begins to feel less motivated. When she expresses her masculine pursuing side, he moves too far to his feminine receptive side. This imbalance slowly erodes the passion in a marriage.

Most men have no idea that too much assertiveness and sexual aggression on a woman's part can eventually turn them off. Some men like a woman's assertiveness very much at first and couldn't say why they find they are no longer attracted to her or suddenly find other women more attractive. In the beginning a sexually assertive woman may feel great for him because he feels relieved that he doesn't have to risk rejections, but over time his passion will lessen.

There is no problem with a woman initiating sex some of the time. It becomes a problem when she initiates sex more of the time. Gradually, he will initiate sex less and lose interest.

JULY 22

Wallets and Purses

Contrasts in the ways Martians and Venusians confront the world are most visually apparent when we compare a woman's purse with a man's wallet. Venusians sometimes carry large, heavy bags with beautiful decorations and shiny colors, while Martians carry lightweight, plain black or brown wallets that are designed to hold only the bare essentials: a driver's license, major credit cards, and paper money.

One can never be too sure what one will find when looking into a woman's purse. Even she may not know. But one thing is for sure: she will be carrying everything she could possibly need, along with whatever others may need too.

To a woman, her purse is her security blanket, a trusted friend, an important part of herself. You can tell how expanded a woman's awareness is by the size of her purse. She is prepared for every emergency, wherever she may find herself.

Interestingly, when she is being escorted to a grand ball, she will leave this purse at home and bring a little shiny purse with the bare essentials. In this case, she feels that this night is for her. She is being taken care of by her man, and she doesn't have to feel responsible for anybody. She feels so special and so supported that she doesn't need the security of her purse.

JULY 23

Patience Is Divine

When our hearts are open, we are patient with our partner's limitations and our own. When strong feelings of impatience appear, they are another signal that childhood feelings are clouding our vision.

As adults, we have learned how to wait patiently for desire to become reality. Patience is a skill and a part of maturity. When we suddenly begin to feel impatient, we lose our realistic perspective and immediately demand more than is possible.

Instead of feeling good that progress is being achieved, we feel frustrated that not enough is happening fast enough. With each setback, we negate our progress.

When a woman becomes impatient, she will demand that her partner make his changes immediately and permanently instead of realizing that he is engaged in an ongoing process to give her the support she needs. Instead of giving up or demanding more, a woman needs to focus less on changing her partner and more on changing her own attitude. Open your heart and pray for patience. It is a divine gift. Asking for patience reminds us that life unfolds in God's time and not ours.

JULY 24

Romantic Getaways

*A*s I have mentioned, one of the simplest and most powerful ways to rekindle passion is to get out of the house on a romantic getaway. Enjoy a change of scenery. Get away from the routine and familiar. Temporarily leave all domestic responsibilities behind. The more beautiful the new environment is, the better.

Try to get away at least one night once a month. If you can't visit a vacation spot or a neighboring town, go to a local hotel. Sometimes just getting into a different bed can do the trick.

Women particularly may need a change of environment to be aroused. This change frees the woman from feeling responsible for the family and the home. When the environment is beautiful, it awakens her to her inner beauty.

JULY 25

Cause and Effect

When we openly or secretly judge another, that person will tend momentarily to become the way we have judged them to be. For example, if we judge them to be unloving, they may become momentarily unloving; if we judge them to be uncaring, they may react in an uncaring way.

The more significant a person is to you, the more you are affected and provoked by their judgments. When you are dependent upon a person, your effect on their thoughts and feelings increases. Being sexually intimate with a person also heightens their impact on your behavior.

JULY 26

How Men Take Credit

When a man takes a woman out, she has a golden opportunity to make him feel special as well. When she appreciates what he provides for her, he feels more intimate with her.

When a man and woman go to a movie and she likes the movie, a part of him takes credit. He feels, "Yes, I wrote that movie, I directed it, and I starred in it." Of course, intellectually he knows he didn't create the movie, but emotionally it is as if he did.

To keep the romance, she can be sensitive to his feelings when she is not happy with a movie. She doesn't need to point out to him in great detail that she didn't like the movie. A man feels most romantic when he feels successful in providing for her happiness.

JULY 27

Taking Time to Heal

When we feel rejected or excluded, it hurts in our hearts. While this pain is not visible like a bruise or cut, it is just as real and takes time to heal. During this healing period we should not expect ourselves to be our most loving selves. While we are healing, it is a time to receive and a time to give more to ourselves. As we fill up with more love, our wounds will heal and once again we will be able to freely share our hearts.

~~~≈≈~~~

Masculine Violence

*P*robably the most negative form of acting out hurt is revenge. When a man is unable to heal his hurt, he generally feels a compulsion to release his hurt by inflicting it on someone else. This is a very important element of the male psyche. Violence is generally the compulsion of the male psyche to release its pain and feel better. Breaking something or someone is a backward or subconscious way of saying "This is what you have done to me." As men learn to communicate more effectively, this tendency gradually lessens.

In a primitive way, when a man is possessed by his pain, he can objectively experience and release it by inflicting it on others. This means that when he can see, hear, or feel the pain of another person, it reflects his own.

> **As men learn to communicate their pain,**
> **they will become less violent.**

The inclination to release pain by hurting back is the basis of all violence and war. As men learn to communicate their pain, they will become less violent. There is a condition that must be met before men can communicate their pain, they must first be able to feel it.

The first and most important step in this process is to learn to listen to a woman's painful feelings. When a man learns to do this, it is much easier for him to get in touch with his own feelings.

Another approach is to join a support group. By hearing others share, he can more effectively look inside and feel his own pain.

JULY 29

~~~

Why a Man's Feelings Change

*W*hen couples move too quickly to experience intimacy, a man doesn't experience again and again how much he wants to be with a woman. In some cases he will realize how special she is to him only when she backs off and stops pursuing him. Quite often a man will pull back, and then—once the woman has let go—spring back with greater desire and love.

This reaction is very confusing to a woman. When he comes back, she often feels it is too late. She is unable to bend back to him because it is hard to believe that his sudden rush of love is real. She feels hurt and is afraid of getting hurt again. She thinks that if she goes back, he will just lose his newfound interest. Without understanding how she contributed to the problem, she can't make sure it doesn't happen again.

With this insight, instead of feeling like a victim at the whim of her partner's changing feelings, she can feel assured that she has the power to get what she needs. She can trust her partner's love when she feels the power to create the right conditions for their love to grow.

꩜

Preparation

*T*o realize our power to create what we need, we must accept that when we are not getting, we are not giving. Or more precisely, we are not giving what our partner needs. To receive more in our relationships, we must learn how to give not what we would need, but what our partner needs. When we succeed in fulfilling their needs, they will spontaneously begin to respond to our support by supporting us in return.

The success of our giving is determined by our partner's willingness to support back. If our partner is unaffected by our gifts, rather than blaming them for being unappreciative, we must be accountable and explore ways we can give more successfully.

When women give too much and don't get back, rather than resenting their partner, they need to reflect on what they are giving and focus on giving him what he really wants. A man would rather a woman give less and be happier than be resentful about giving more. When a woman is happier, she is able to give a man the appreciation and acceptance he hungers for.

Men and Feelings

*T*o begin to develop the ability to communicate pain in a safe way, a man needs to listen to the pain of others who have suffered similar injustice. In hearing the pain of others, he is able to feel, share, and heal his own pain without taking revenge. As a result, he becomes more capable of hearing a woman's pain. He becomes more compassionate and understanding.

It is important to point out that when a man is incapable of being compassionate, this does not mean he does not care about his partner. When a man becomes detached, a woman often assumes that he doesn't care about her hurt.

In truth, he does care but becomes detached because he is getting in touch with his resistance to feeling his own pain. His apparent resistance to her is not a sign of his uncaring but of his inability to feel his own emotions. As men learn to listen and then feel and communicate their own hurt, they can be free of their automatic resistance to hearing or sharing feelings.

❧ AUGUST ❧

Create, Achieve, Empower

*L*ove empowers us, and people who are empowered can create and achieve wonderful things.

When a woman enlists the support of a man, she empowers him to be all that he can be. A man feels empowered when he is trusted, accepted, appreciated, admired, approved of, and encouraged.

A man empowers a woman by creating a place of security for her. Within it, she can achieve all her dreams and desires. A woman feels empowered when she is cared for, understood, respected, cherished, validated, and reassured.

Often we are not able to empower our partners because of negative judgments we hold about ourselves. Negative judgments keep us from fully enjoying all we have in our lives. Ultimately, negative judgments can ruin relationships.

To empower ourselves, we must first release our negative judgments of others. By loving others, we are able to love ourselves; by loving ourselves, we can love others. In other words, by empowering others, we empower ourselves.

AUGUST 1

※

The Power of Love

*W*hen our hearts are open and we love, respect, and appreciate our partners, we are capable of supporting them even when they are not as perfect as we might have thought in earlier stages. Spiritual chemistry gives us the power to overcome the judgments, doubts, demands, and criticism we may sometimes experience. Even if our hearts temporarily close down, we can more easily find our way back to that love with the solid foundation of many loving and positive experiences.

By repeatedly coming back to love, you will eventually gain the confidence and self-assurance necessary to pick your special partner for life. Instead of going through the power struggles many couples experience, you will be able to draw on that spiritual chemistry to find the right compromise, to apologize when necessary, and to forgive your partner for not being perfect.

꙳ꙮ꙳

The Art of Empowering a Man

*J*ust as men need to learn the art of listening to fulfill a woman's primary love needs, women need to learn the art of empowerment. When a woman enlists the support of a man, she empowers him to be all that he can be. A man feels empowered when he is trusted, accepted, appreciated, admired, approved of, and encouraged. Any attempt to change him takes away the loving trust, acceptance, appreciation, admiration, approval, and encouragement that are his primary needs.

The secret of empowering a man is never to try to change him or improve him. Certainly you may want him to change—just don't act on that desire. Only if he directly and specifically asks for advice is he open to assistance in changing. Another approach is to pray. By asking God to support our partner, we are released from that burden. Not only are the angels in heaven happy to be of service but your partner will be happier as well.

⁓⁕⁓

How We Influence Each Other

*W*hen men and women begin to understand their differences in a new and positive light, learn each other's language, and practice new relationship skills, they are able to draw from their partner the best they have to offer. As a result, men and women are more fulfilled.

A man is greatly fulfilled because he feels successful in supporting his partner, and a woman feels fulfilled because she has created a relationship in which to grow and thrive. They may still speak different languages, but harmony grows as they begin learning how to translate and correctly convey important messages.

When a woman can understand a man's behavior and is able to express a greater acceptance of him, over time he begins to change and become more attentive. Her nondemanding attitude draws him out into the relationship like a magnet.

When a man begins to duck and dodge by correctly interpreting his partner's feelings, he is able to listen to her with greater empathy and comprehension. At the most basic level of her being, she feels seen, heard, understood, and supported. Her feminine spirit soars. As a result, she is able to be more loving and accepting of him. As he increasingly understands her, he quite naturally begins to share more with her.

While these skills may seem unnatural in the beginning, in time they will become automatic. They are merely the extensions of social and language skills we have already been using for centuries.

AUGUST 4

What Men Need

A man is empowered and nurtured most when he feels appreciated, accepted, and trusted. To a man, sex is so important because when a woman is aroused, she is actually giving him a megadose of what he needs most.

When a woman is longing to have sex with a man, she is most open and trusting. In a very dramatic way, she is willing to surrender her defenses and not only reveal her nakedness but bring him into her body and being as well. By desiring a man in this way, she makes him feel truly accepted. When his every touch creates a pleasurable response, he feels greatly appreciated. In the most tangible and physical way possible, he feels and experiences that he is making a difference.

Like a thirsty man wandering in the desert,
in sex a man can finally relax
and take a drink from the oasis of his feelings.

Even if he is stressed from the day, if his wife is feeling loved and supported and enjoys sex with him, he can be immediately rejuvenated. Although it seems as if sex makes him feel better, it is really that he is feeling again and able to let in her love. He is no longer cut off from his feeling self but can move into that deserted part of his being again. He can feel whole again. Like a thirsty man wandering in the desert, he can finally relax and take a drink from the oasis of his feelings.

꼬리장식

Giving Up Judgments

*A*s we become able to understand our differences and successfully communicate our feelings, thoughts, and desires, we can then begin to let go of our negative judgments. Our negative appraisals of ourselves and the results of our actions inhibit us from fully expressing our talents. Ultimately, deprecatory judgments keep us from fully enjoying our lives and all we have.

> ***In general, judgment and criticism***
> ***are symptoms of low self-esteem.***

When we feel that we are not enough, we begin to feel that what we have or what belongs to us is not enough. We do not have enough time, money, love—whatever. We begin to feel that friends or family are not enough. Negative judgments ruin our relationships.

Judgment will continue until we understand, appreciate, and honor the differences between people. When we are able to accept, appreciate, and respect others, quite automatically we begin to accept and appreciate ourselves. This is the true secret of releasing judgment. By loving others, we are able to love ourselves, and by loving ourselves, we can love others. Our self-esteem and self-worth grow daily when we are creating loving relationships. It is a gradual process of growing in love.

~≈≈~

When the Clock Keeps Ticking and He's Not Wearing a Watch

*M*arriage is to women what sex is to men. If a woman told a man she only wanted to go to second base with him, he would instinctively feel something was missing. He would want to go all the way sexually. Similarly, a woman wants to go all the way emotionally and get married. It is a common tragedy—a woman wants to get married and a man doesn't want to take that step.

Fortunately, there is an alternative to giving an ultimatum or denying one's need: a woman can move back a stage. Instead of being in stage five—engagement—and demanding that her partner move on with her, she can move back to stage four—intimacy—and share how she feels in a nondemanding way without blaming him. Men respond much better when they are seen not as the problem but as the solution.

She could say something like this: "I find myself at times pulling away and I wanted you to know my feelings. I am so happy in our relationship that I begin to feel a desire to get married and have a family. I don't know how you feel about this, but the last thing I would want to do is tell you what to do or make a demand. I am not sure if you are ready to move in that direction, so I think a part of me is beginning to wonder if this is the right relationship for me.

Anyway, I wanted you to know why sometimes I seem withdrawn. I am just working through a variety of feelings. Thanks for listening." This kind of nondemanding message is honest and lets him feel his natural motivation to make a shift if he is ready.

AUGUST 7

To Ask or Not to Ask

*I*t used to be that the squeaky wheel got the grease. Today the squeaky wheel gets replaced. Asking for more can easily begin to sound like nagging. Men hate to hear it, and women hate to do it. Without understanding how to help a man learn to listen to her feelings, a woman is left with only two alternatives. She can become a martyr and settle for whatever she gets, or she can try demanding and nagging for more.

Neither alternative will work. To get the love and support she needs, a woman must focus on what is most essential. Ask him just to listen and not to feel pressure to change in any way. Gradually over time, as he understands her feelings better, she can begin to ask for more support.

Illness

One way of viewing illness is to recognize it as an expression of unhealed psychological pain. Sometimes disease is the self punishing itself through the body. From this perspective, illness and disease are manifestations of the dark side of our female self. Just as the male side punishes externally, the female side punishes internally.

In a positive sense, the male side of us is responsible for being of service to others, while the female side of us is responsible for self-healing and personal growth. By hearing the pain of our female self, we heal our tendency toward sickness and suffering. Quite often, really good and loving people get sick. This can be the result of not being open to receiving support in their lives. Sometimes the best at giving are the worst at receiving. Giving and not receiving must eventually take its toll on the body.

August 9

Women Give What Women Want

*W*hen a man receives from a woman, it opens him up to receive more, but when a woman receives from a man, it opens her up to give more. Without this insight about our different reactions, a woman will automatically give what she would want and assume that it will make a man more interested in her.

If a man were to listen attentively to her, she would definitely become more interested in him. If a man were to notice her needs and wishes and happily go out of his way to fulfill them, then she would be swept off her feet. The opposite is not true. When a woman listens to a man, often he becomes more interested in himself. When a woman goes out of her way for a man, he relaxes and wonders what he did to deserve such wonderful treatment.

August 10

Different Interests Create Chemistry

*S*ingle people mistakenly assume that their soul mate will share all their interests. As a result, they look for partners with similar interests. They don't realize that there are hundreds, even thousands, of places to find their soul mate.

**There is greater physical chemistry
when your partner has different interests.**

Certainly it is possible to find a soul mate who shares our interests, but it is just as possible to find one among people who are interested in things that do not interest us. When couples are happily married, it is not because of common interests. Different interests actually fuel lasting attraction. What allows them to harmonize and respect their differences is shared values and good communication.

August 11

Finding Our Oneness

*T*rue relationship is born from an awareness and appreciation of how we are different. From the vantage point of understanding and respecting our differences, we can more clearly appreciate our similarities. Recognizing our similarities gives rise to such positive attitudes as compassion, empathy, understanding, acceptance, tolerance, and oneness. Acknowledging our differences creates attraction, appreciation, interest, respect, purposefulness, and excitement.

As we succeed in understanding each other through honest sharing and heartfelt listening, we begin to realize and release the negative judgments that separate us from one another. We see that it is not differences that separate us, but our judgments about those differences—judgments born out of misunderstanding.

AUGUST 12

Sharing Your Love

*W*hen men and women fail in relationships, it is not because they are not loving. We are all born with love in our hearts and a purpose to fulfill. We experience pain in our relationships because we do not know how to share our love in ways that work. We are missing relationship skills.

Sometimes love is not expressed because it is buried deep inside, locked within the fortress of our hearts. Hiding behind a wall, we are safe from hurt but barred from love.

So many people are imprisoned in themselves. They do not know how to find their love so that they can share it. Endless opportunities to love are wasted in a lifetime when we are not taught the basic skills for communicating and relating in a loving manner.

The Power of Attitude

A man's interest in a woman can grow only when he feels actively interested. On the other hand, his interest will tend to decline slowly if he only feels receptively interested in her.

When a man is actively interested in a woman, it gives her an opportunity to explore her true and authentic responses to his pursuit. This authenticity makes her more attractive to the right kind of guy for her. With this understanding, dating can be the ultimate opportunity to explore and access the potential of a relationship while having a good time.

If a woman pursues a man with active interest, it makes him receptively interested. Athough he likes receiving her interest, warmth, and affection, it does not make him more interested in her. Receptive interest just does not bring out the best in a man. After a while, he becomes interested in someone else who does promise to bring out the best in him.

These same principles apply in a marriage. When a man becomes too passive, it makes a woman more active. Eventually she begins to resent him. In a similar fashion, when a woman becomes more actively interested in making the relationship work, it can make the man more passive and less interested in her and the relationship. With this insight, we can work to find balance and sustain a loving and lasting relationship.

꧁꧂

Love and Submission

*M*any people confuse submission with love: "If she loves me, she will do what I want" or "I will do it because I love you, even though I really don't want to do it." A surefire way to kill the love in a relationship is to sacrifice your wants and needs in order to be loved by someone else. When you stop caring about yourself and your needs, there are no longer two people in the relationship. It's hard to be interested in nobody.

Through compromise we can make sacrifices in the name of love without sacrificing who we are.

To love another doesn't mean you make them more important than yourself. There is nothing more boring than being in a relationship with someone who feels they have no self-worth. You are mistaken if you think that you will impress your partner by treating them as if they are better than you are. If you care more about your partner than yourself, one day you will find that your partner feels the same.

※※

Negative Self-Talk

*T*he main way a woman hurts herself is subjectively. She abuses herself with negative self-talk. As a result, she may decide to punish or deprive herself. The major symptom of negative self-talk is a feeling of unworthiness, helplessness, and self-pity. With self-pity, she denies her power to create more in her life and indirectly blames others, affirming her powerlessness.

For example, she may say in self-pity, "No one appreciates me; no one knows how hard I work and how much I sacrifice." In affirming "poor me," she is denying her inner potential to be happy and improve her life. In this way, self-pity is a form of inner violence. Just as outward violence inhibits another's potential to be happy, through self-pity we restrict our own ability to be happy.

As women learn to feel and release their hurt without self-pity and resentment and consequently receive the compassion they need, they can gradually release the tendency to feel self-pity. In a similar but opposite way, as men learn to share their pain and understand the pain of others, they gradually release the tendency to be mean or violent.

❧❦❧

Don't Say, "Well, I Disagree. I Think . . . "

Sometimes women feel that the only way to be heard is to disagree. It's fine to disagree, but don't express your disagreement as an interruption. Instead, say something like "I have another take on this . . ." or "I have another way of looking at that . . ."

These statements are gracious, and they make a man receptive to what a woman has to say, as well as intrigued. She is saying, "I think what you are saying has merit, and I have something different to say about it." Rather than getting defensive about his point of view, he is intrigued to hear what else can be said.

A man is turned on by a woman who is able to express her point of view graciously. A woman should not agree with a man just to appear nice and sweet. That's a surefire way to kill attraction. By learning to express her disagreement in a more fluid, feminine manner, a woman will find it becomes easier to set boundaries and sustain a different point of view without the fear of losing love.

❦

Healing the Resentment Flu

*R*esentment, like getting the flu or a cold, is not healthy. When a woman is sick with resentment, she tends to negate what a man has done for her because, according to the way she keeps score, she has done so much more.

When the score is forty to ten in favor of the woman, she may begin to feel very resentful. Something happens to a woman when she feels she is giving more than she is getting. Quite unconsciously, she subtracts his score of ten from her score of forty and concludes that the score in their relationship is thirty to zero. This makes sense mathematically and is understandable, but it doesn't work.

When she subtracts his score from her score, he ends up with a zero, and he is not a zero. He has not given zero; he has given ten. When he comes home, she has a coldness in her eyes or in her voice that says he is a zero. She is negating what he has done. She reacts to him as if he has given nothing, but he has given ten.

What generally happens in a relationship at this point is that the man feels unappreciated and loses his motivation to do more. He catches the resentment flu. Then she continues to feel more resentful and the situation gets worse and worse.

*With resentment flu a woman
begins to negate all that a man has done for her.*

The way to solve this problem is to understand it compassionately from both sides. He needs to be appreciated, while she needs to feel supported. Otherwise their sickness will get worse.

The solution to this resentment is for her to take responsibility. She needs to take responsibility for having contributed to her problem by giving more and letting the score get so uneven. She needs to treat herself as if she has the flu or a cold and take a rest from giving so much in the relationship. She needs to pamper herself and allow her partner to take care of her more.

A man can release his own resentment by understanding that she needs to receive for a while before she can give again. He can remember this as he attentively gives his love and affection in little ways. For a while, he should not expect her to be as appreciative as he deserves and needs her to be. It helps if he takes responsibility for giving her the flu by neglecting to do the little things that she needs.

With this foresight, he can give without expecting much in return until she recovers from her flu. Knowing that he can solve this problem will help him release his resentment as well. If he continues giving and she focuses on taking a rest from giving and focuses on receiving his support with love, that balance can be quickly restored.

Learning through Listening

*T*he better we can learn to understand our different reactions to and needs under stress, the more hope we can feel for our relationships as well as for the world. As men learn to listen to the feelings of women, they become more aware of their own feelings; they become more compassionate, caring, understanding, and respectful of women. As women feel this compassion, they are able to share more of themselves and heal their hurts in a journey of increasing love, trust, acceptance, forgiveness, gratitude, appreciation, and empowerment.

By learning to take care of ourselves at times of stress rather than demanding that our partners fix us, we release the impulse to make others responsible for us. We then enjoy the beautiful experience of feeling responsible to be all we can be along with the confidence that we can skillfully support the ones we love, especially in times of stress.

꙳꙳

When and How to Practice the Anger Process

*W*henever you are feeling down, somewhere in your subconscious you are blaming yourself. Anger allows you to bring those feelings up and out and so uncover your inner love and power.

The anger process has three steps:

1. Express anger and blame at yourself. (Use "you" statements—direct the anger out.)

2. Express what you want. (Use "I want" statements.)

3. Express positive, loving, supportive statements.

This process can be even more effective if you don't do it with a partner. To do it with a partner, imagine that your partner is you and begin expressing your anger and blame. Your partner then repeats back every sentence.

The powerful and energizing result of this process can only be experienced; it can't be described or imagined. The next time you want to feel better, more awake, more alive, more powerful, or more expressive, then find something about yourself at which to get angry. By eventually releasing this anger with love, you will feel much better.

If you can't find anything to be angry about, make up something or remember something from your past. If you are in a situation where it is inappropriate to express such feelings, you can write them out. Some people tape the anger process and play it on their way to work, repeating back every sentence. Remember when you make the recording to leave space on the tape for these repetitions.

AUGUST 20

A Time for Hope

*P*erhaps for the first time in history, we are entering a phase when love can be mastered. This millennial time is one of great hope for relationships and the world. Previously on our planet, survival was the guiding purpose. Slowly but surely, in the last several thousand years, love has become increasingly important. It can become a guiding force within us all. The widespread dissatisfaction between men and women in relationships is a symptom that the world wants more. The pain of nations is the pain we feel when we can't share our love.

We no longer turn away from our deeper feelings. We hunger deep in our hearts to love. This shift has already taken place. The love is already there. Although we are born with the ability to love, it is a skill that still must be learned. As we begin to understand how to love others, we are truly paving the way to a better and more loving world. When we can live in love, there is hope for our world.

AUGUST 21

❧

Bringing Out the Best in Her

*E*very man has the power to bring out the best in a woman, but only a few men realize it. If a man could see himself through a woman's eyes, he would experience what makes him irresistible to her. He would clearly see the attributes he already has that really turn a woman on. It is almost impossible for a man to see himself this way. He doesn't recognize that what a woman wants most, he already has.

It is easy to conclude that a man is most attractive to a woman because he has a great personality or because he is very talented, handsome, friendly, funny, witty, strong, entertaining, rich, successful, wise, or interesting. Regardless of any of these traits, what makes a man most attractive to a woman is his ability to make her feel like a woman. When he is attentive, interested, playful, and caring, she is most easily swept off her feet and able to recognize and appreciate his admirable qualities.

Empowering Forgiveness

Understanding how our thoughts and feelings can provoke a reaction does not mean we should condone or excuse the provoked behavior. It simply gives us a way to understand our partner's behavior; it creates an opening through which we can more fully relate to their reaction.

Just as judgments provoke temporary dysfunction, resentments provoke continuous dysfunction. A man who resents his wife's emotions may provoke her into being continuously hypersensitive. A woman who resents her husband's uncaring attitude may provoke him into being continuously indifferent.

When we resent, we are holding on to our negative judgments. They stay firmly rooted until we experience some forgiveness. When we are unable to release our judgments, their power to provoke increases. No matter how good you think you are at disguising resentment, it is revealed in your actions, reactions, choice of words, body language, eyes, and tone of voice.

> *No matter how good you think you are at disguising resentment, it will seep out whether you are aware of it or not.*

If you are free of resentment and you begin to judge a person negatively, that judgment can easily be replaced minutes later with a positive judgment. When you feel resentful, you are actually holding on to that judgment either consciously or unconsciously.

Accumulated resentment undermines the growth of love in a relationship. The first step toward releasing resentment is to claim your responsibility to understand how you provoke the responses you get. With a greater understanding of your partner and with better communication, forgiveness will become easier.

AUGUST 23

What Happens When You Love Yourself

When you love yourself in the presence of others, you are able to express your inner gifts and talents without fear or restriction. The more you love yourself, the more you are able to come out. The more you come out, the easier it is for people to appreciate the real you and not the image you project or the mask you wear. The more people appreciate and love you, the more you can love yourself. It is a cycle of increasing love and true self-expression.

When you don't love yourself and you mask your real self, the cycle works in the opposite direction of decreasing love and true self-expression.

Loving yourself more gives you the ability to love and appreciate others more as well. The world becomes a different place. For each of us, the world is a big mirror, showing us a reflection of who we are. We each see the world through different-colored glasses, determined by the way we feel about ourselves.

AUGUST 24

❧❧

Making the Choice to Respond

*I*t is crucial that a man experience repeatedly that he can make and is making a difference in a woman's life. Men always thrive in a relationship when they feel needed and appreciated. When a woman can respond to the little things he does, then his affection, attraction, and interest have a chance to grow.

As a woman learns to respond to men with each of these three attributes of femininity—being self-assured, receptive, and responsive—she is able to be most attractive to men.

A Healthy Relationship

*W*e sometimes need to be reminded that when we relate with real love, we see ourselves in our partners. With this feeling of connectedness and oneness, we automatically receive back when we support their needs. By giving with an open heart (or with real love), we experience the greatest joy in our lives.

When loving is not joyful, then we are confused about love. When love is difficult or a strain, we are demanding that our partner fix us. So many of us confuse love with needing. We get things backward. We assume that being loved means having one's needs fulfilled. In reality, we feel the greatest love as adults when our love is being received.

~~~~~~

Learning to Become Resentment Free

You may wish to be loving—you may even try with all your might—but your love will never be pure unless you are free from resentment. When we are free from resentment, loving is effortless. When we have to try hard to love, this is generally a sign that we are repressing our resentments.

If a positive attitude is not automatic and effortless, then it is fabricated. When we feel resentful, there is no way we can hide it from the listener. It will always put listeners on guard to protect themselves from our blame.

With this knowledge about resentment, it is easier to be more responsible in our relationships. We become capable of taking responsibility when we recognize how our negative judgments, hidden or expressed, actually provoke much of the resistance or lack of support we get.

꩜

Creating Change

*I*t is important to schedule special occasions. A man needs to remember that women tend to feel the weight of domestic responsibility and find it hard to take time off for themselves. If he creates special times when she can get out of the routine, she is free to feel nurtured.

Celebrations, parties, presents, and cards also affirm the passage of time. They are particularly important for women. A woman greatly appreciates a man's special attention to her at these times. His remembering birthdays, anniversaries, Valentine's Day, and other holidays means a lot to a woman. Doing something special for her on those days frees her from feeling overwhelmed by life's repetitive responsibilities and assures her that she is loved.

One of the chief passion assassins is routine. Even if you are comfortable in your rut, it is helpful to break out of it from time to time. Even doing silly things can help make a moment special and memorable.

Ultimately what keeps passion alive in a relationship is growing in love. When as a result of living, laughing, crying, and learning together two people are able to love and trust each other more, the passion will continue.

～～～

Verbal Reassurance

*E*very day a woman needs to receive some form of verbal reassurance that she is loved. This means saying things like "I love you, I love you, I love you, I love you, I love you, I love you, I love you." There is basically one way to say it, and it needs to be said over and over.

Men sometimes stop saying "I love you" because they want to be new and original. They imagine that a woman would grow tired of it or become bored by it. But saying "I love you" is never redundant. Saying it is actually a process of allowing her to feel his love. He may love her, but if he doesn't say it she won't feel it. One way a man can relate to this is by comparing the simple statement "I love you" with a phrase that he never tires of hearing. That phrase is "Thank you." Rarely does a man weary of being told "Thank you" after he has done something for someone.

Another phrase that is very validating for a woman is "I understand." If (and only if) a man does understand, then it is very helpful to say this out loud. When a man says "I understand," a woman is assured that she has been heard. A complimentary phrase that men appreciate is "That makes sense." When a man hears "That makes sense," he feels equally supported.

~≈≈~

A Woman's Worth

*W*ithout an understanding of men, many women think they have to do something to earn a man's love and attention. These women do not understand the intrinsic value of simply being interested in and receptive to what a man has to offer. A woman does not recognize that being open and responsive to what a man is doing is in itself giving back to the man.

A woman thrives when a man does for her. When a man is actively interested, she is most interested in him. Since this is her experience, she mistakenly assumes it is the same for a man, but it is not. A man is impressed more by how a woman responds to him than by what she does or can do for him.

Most women don't realize their value to men. A man thrives when a woman is open and receptive to his interests and his attempts to impress and fulfill her. Her receptivity is her gift to him. He is grateful for the opportunity to know her, connect with her, and bask in her radiance. Without her to please, he is a man out of work. He needs a job, he needs the opportunity to succeed in a relationship with a woman. This is an enormous boost to his fulfillment in life.

AUGUST 30

Discovering Our Purpose

*A*s human beings, we are all purposeful. The more we understand and accept our male and female energies, the more able we are to discover the sacred treasure of knowing who we are and what we are able to do. We can unlock this treasure chest by exploring the male and female energies within us. This exploration leads to greater understanding, which opens the door to greater self-esteem, self-worth, confidence, happiness, and peace.

AUGUST 31

Change and Grow

*O*ver time, living with the same person can eventually become very boring if they are not regularly changing. Staying fresh is crucial for both partners in a marriage. Just as listening to a favorite song a hundred times in a row makes it grow stale, so may our partners become boring if they do not grow and change.

Just as physical growth is so obvious in our children, we must always continue to grow emotionally, mentally, and spiritually. We must be careful not to sacrifice or deny ourselves too much. When a relationship does not allow us to grow, the passion between two people begins to fade.

Loving your partner does not mean spending all your time together. Too much time together can make a relationship commonplace and devoid of mystery. Enjoying other friends and activities means that you can always bring back something new to the relationship. A healthy relationship requires a balance of doing things separately from your partner, doing things with your partner and others, and then doing things privately and intimately, just the two of you.

❧ SEPTEMBER ❧

Knowledge, Expression, Balance

September is the time to harvest the knowledge and love you have gained from sharing your lives together. Quite often we don't realize how much we have grown unless we take some time to reflect on what we have been through. This is a time to sit back and appreciate the love you have created and let go of any old resentments.

Knowing how much to give and how much to ask for is an ongoing process. It is never clearly black or white. When we begin to feel we have been giving too much, we must come back to setting our limits and asking for the support that is dear to us.

Though it is important to receive the support we need and deserve, we must always remember that it is in giving love that we are most fulfilled. To experience true love is a special blessing. It is easy to take it for granted and get lost in petty complaints. The joy of loving is that we can always forgive our partner and start again, when we feel some imbalance has occurred.

When our partner's imperfections show up, it is easy to forget that they are really doing their best and that they truly love us. By reflecting on their efforts, our hearts soften and we appreciate what we do receive. The love and caring we feel for our partner not only nurtures them but gives our lives direction and purpose.

SEPTEMBER 1

～☙❧～

What Are You Really Feeling?

*R*epressing your feelings is a safety mechanism. While we are growing up, when we are unable to cope with and express the truth about our emotions, we learn to hide those feelings deep inside and hope they just go away. Through the years of rejecting and suppressing our authentic feelings, we acquire the unfortunate and unhealthy habit of automatically repressing any unsafe, unacceptable, or confusing emotions.

We learn to experience only those feelings that won't disturb or threaten our lives or those of others, ensuring safety and acceptance. We become strangers to our own feelings. We begin to figure out in our heads what to feel rather than feeling simply and spontaneously from our hearts.

Locating buried emotions is absolutely essential to growth because to the extent that we suppress and bury our feelings, we will lose contact with who we are and what we really want. We may think we want many things, but they don't bring lasting happiness because they are not our soul's desire. As we learn to connect with our true feelings, our lives become richer and more fulfilling, although there are more ups and downs.

Stress Management for Men and Women

*T*he complementary viewpoints, objectivity and subjectivity, are two ways to decrease stress. The masculine way to reduce stress is to change or eliminate whatever object or situation is causing the stress. The feminine way is to adjust one's attitude so that one is not affected in a stressful way. Women tend to change the belief or attitude causing the stress.

Changing one's behavior is the masculine way to reduce stress, improving the situation by doing something differently. Our feminine side reduces stress by changing attitudes—to improve the situation through forgiveness, love, gratitude, or tolerance. Both approaches used together bring about the most positive and powerful result.

꙳꙳

When a Man Is on His Female Side

A man needs to be careful not to look to a woman to fulfill his feminine needs. Ideally, a man should look to a woman primarily to nurture his male side and not his female side. His male side is nurtured every time he feels appreciated, accepted, and trusted. The more nurtured he feels, the stronger and tougher he will be, but he will grow more sensitive to her needs at the same time. This sensitivity to her needs is what women really appreciate, and it makes him feel strong and loving.

If he happens to be more sensitive than she is, it may take a few years to balance out and find his masculine strength in the relationship. In the meantime, he should not burden her with his sensitivities. For example, if his feelings are hurt, or if he feels more emotionally needy, he should talk with men friends and not look to her primarily to support his need to talk and share feelings.

SEPTEMBER 4

When Martians Don't Talk

*T*he biggest challenge for a woman is to interpret and support a man when he isn't talking. Silence is most easily misinterpreted by women.

Quite often a man will suddenly stop communicating and become silent. This is unheard of on Venus. At first a woman may think the man is deaf. She thinks that maybe he doesn't hear what's being said, and that is why he is not responding.

Before men talk or respond, they first silently mull over what they have heard or experienced. Internally and silently they figure out the most correct or useful response. They first formulate it internally and then express it. This process could take from minutes to hours. To make matters even more confusing for women, if a man does not have enough information to process an answer, he may not respond at all.

Women need to understand that when a man is silent, he is saying, "I don't know what to say yet, but I am thinking about it." While a man is mulling something over, it is nearly impossible for him to hear what is being said around him. He may be hearing sounds, but his mind is focused on what he is thinking about and temporarily can't take in more information.

~~~

How Women Go Out of Balance

*W*hat typically happens in a relationship is that a woman will tend to compromise and adjust herself continually to preserve harmony and avoid confrontation. On a conscious level, she will try to change herself. After she has sacrificed or surrendered her position repeatedly, she will begin to feel resentful that her partner is not doing the same. On a less conscious level, she will begin to try to change her partner. All communication at this point becomes somewhat manipulative and very distasteful to him. He will inevitably reject her or rebel.

A woman shifts into manipulating when her first means of getting what she needs fails. Her problem is that no one ever taught her what to change about herself to get what she needs. To change herself does not mean to give herself up; it does not mean to act a certain way. The emphasis is not on changing her behavior and speech but on changing her attitudes. By releasing resentment and mistrust, she will automatically begin getting more of what she wants and also enjoy expressing her true and loving self.

SEPTEMBER 6

Labor and Love

A man can be stressed out from a day at work, but if his partner is happy with him, he feels fulfilled. When he senses her appreciation of his labor, his stress level dissipates.

> ***A woman's appreciation is a shower***
> ***that washes away the stressful grime of a man's day.***

When an exhausted woman returns home to a happy man, he doesn't make her day. It's great that he appreciates her hard work to help support the family, but it doesn't in the least diminish her stress. As we have discussed, she needs to communicate and feel some nurturing support before she can begin to feel better.

By understanding and honoring that men thrive on appreciation and women on communication, we gain the knowledge and the power to create mutually fulfilling relationships.

꘡꘡

Why Men Appear Self-Centered

*A*n example of psychological contraction in men is a source of great confusion for women. It is hard for a woman to understand how a man can love her so attentively and then suddenly shift and appear self-centered. Since this kind of shift is foreign to her, she takes it personally.

She does not realize how automatic it is for a man to become completely oblivious to everyone outside his focus. When he is focused on pleasing her, he is very attentive to her. When he thinks she is pleased, he finds a new focus, like a problem at work, and then directs all his attention to that.

When under stress, men commonly increase their focus and become even more unmindful of others. This creates the appearance that they are self-absorbed or uncaring. At such times, they are not necessarily narcissistic or selfish but may appear that way.

> **Men become absorbed in achieving their goals**
> **and forget everything else.**

To recognize that they really are caring, note that many times the goals they are absorbed in achieving are ultimately very altruistic or supportive of others.

Maturity Means Greater Wisdom

*A*s we become more mature, we gain greater wisdom and self-control. If we have negative addictive habits, eventually we feel motivated to clean up our lives. We start reaching out to get support from others who are getting their lives in order.

By attending various support groups, you have an opportunity to experience the chemistry that comes from shared maturity. There are all kinds of support groups. There are church-sponsored groups, Parents Without Partners groups, Alcoholics Anonymous groups, and so on. All of these places are excellent for making new friends who will open up many new doors to finding your soul mate.

SEPTEMBER 9

Misinterpreting a Woman's Being Overwhelmed

*J*ust as a man becomes completely absorbed in one problem, a woman becomes overwrought by a multitude of problems. One of the ironies of a woman's being overwhelmed is that she temporarily loses her ability to prioritize, which leads to being more overwhelmed. She feels overly responsible, even compelled, to do everything and then feels powerless to do it all. This gives rise to the ancient adage a woman's work is never done.

Without an understanding of this feminine vulnerability, men react to overwhelmed women by becoming frustrated. A man feels that he is being blamed for her unhappiness or that he is somehow responsible for the upset feelings she is experiencing. He defends himself by making her feel wrong for being so overwhelmed, judging her as "making a big deal out of nothing."

Men need to understand that when women are overwhelmed, they are not necessarily trying to accuse or blame; they are just trying to talk about their problems in order to feel better. At times like these, a woman really needs to be heard and not corrected.

When under too much pressure, men and women help themselves feel better in different ways. Women undergoing stress feel better by talking about their problems and being heard, while men feel better by prioritizing their problems, focusing on one, and then developing a plan of action or a solution.

September 10

You Don't Have to Say Anything

*P*robably the most potent and powerful phrase a woman can say to prepare a man to listen is "You don't have to say anything." This message is important because it lets a man off the hook of needing to defend himself. In addition, it gently reminds him that he doesn't have to solve her problems.

A woman would generally not think of this, because with other women it would be rude to say "You don't have to say anything." When women talk on Venus, tradition commands that after one speaks, it is the other's turn to talk. The unspoken agreement is "If I listen to you talk for five minutes, you must listen to me for five minutes."

With a man, it is different. If she says, "You don't have to say anything," he will not find it rude—quite the contrary, he will be relieved. It is an easy job description.

September 11

Feelings Are Your Friends

*T*he ability to feel emotion is a gift we all share as human beings. Often you may not like what you are feeling, but every emotion has a purpose, and that emotion will remain with you until that purpose is realized and understood. Your feelings are like messengers from your subconscious to your conscious mind. Until you receive the message, the messenger will stand patiently at your door.

These are the messages the four healing feelings bring to you:

Anger arises to tell you that what has happened is not what you wanted. A change or adjustment is required.

Sadness arises to tell you that you have lost or are missing something you wanted or needed. Acceptance is required.

Fear arises to warn you of the possibility of failure, loss, or pain. Concern and consideration are required.

Sorrow arises to tell you that you are powerless to change something that you wish you could change. Letting go is required.

The way to understand your emotions and what they are telling you about your life is to feel, explore, and express them. You cannot understand what remains unexpressed.

Have you ever noticed that just by talking about a problem with a friend, you realize the solution? By expressing the complete truth about all your feelings, you can eventually realize the love and understanding underneath all your negative emotions.

~~~~~

Balance through Attraction

*G*enerally speaking, femininity is warm, receptive, vulnerable, feeling, loving, and yielding, while masculinity is cool, aggressive, assertive, reasonable, goal oriented, and decisive. When a man possesses any of these masculine traits, he will seek balance by loving a woman who possesses some of the complementary feminine traits.

> **By loving a woman's feminine qualities,**
> **a man automatically becomes**
> **more accepting of his own feminine side.**

By touching her softness, he awakens to his own softness and yet remains solid. His coolness is balanced by her warmth, his aggression by her receptivity, his assertiveness by her vulnerability, his power by her love, and so on. By this process, he becomes whole. Loving her, he discovers within himself his own feminine qualities. In a similar manner, as she loves him, she begins to feel her masculine qualities.

This paradox is integral to any loving and passionate relationship. By virtue of being different from our partners, we are attracted to them. Through our inner potential to be like them, we are able to relate and have the possibility of intimacy, communication, and closeness.

SEPTEMBER 13

When Women Can't Be Venusian

*F*or a woman to restrict herself by talking only the way a man does goes against her instincts. It eventually prevents her from coping successfully with stress and disconnects her from the warm, open, loving, and feminine feelings that allow her to trust, accept, and appreciate life.

It is very helpful for men to remember that women are instinctively suited to use communication as a means of sorting out their thoughts, clarifying their priorities, and exploring their feelings. Early on in history, women learned to cope with life's problems by talking all day and into the evening with other women. A woman's security was assured by talking and forming alliances and friendships. Just the act of talking brings up an instinctual feeling of security.

With this increased security, she begins to think more clearly and can sort things out much more effectively and in a loving way. In a very real sense, talking for women is like a pump that generates greater clarity. By helping her to speak Venusian, he gives her a precious gift.

～━━～

Attraction Needs Polarity

*W*hen partners do not respect and appreciate their complementary differences, they lose their electricity; they are no longer turned on by each other. Without the polarity, they lose the attraction.

This loss of attraction can happen in two ways. We either suppress our true inner self in an attempt to please our partner, or we try to mold them into our own image. Either strategy— to repress ourselves or to change our partner—will sabotage the relationship.

When we succeed in changing our partner, we may get some short-term need fulfilled, but ultimately there will be no passion. The success of any relationship lies in helping our partners to be true to themselves and making sure we are true to ourselves. When we make compromises, we make sure that eventually we get what we want and express who we are.

SEPTEMBER 15

❧❦❧

Sharing Responsibility

*G*ood communication requires participation on both sides. A man needs to work at remembering that complaining about problems does not mean blaming and that when a woman complains, she is generally just letting go of her frustrations by talking about them. A woman can work at letting him know that although she is complaining, she also appreciates him.

A woman may not think of giving appreciation, because she assumes a man knows how much she appreciates being heard. He doesn't know. When she is talking about problems, he needs to be reassured that he is still loved and appreciated.

Men feel frustrated by problems unless they are doing something to solve them. By appreciating him, a woman can help him realize that just by listening he is also helping.

A woman does not have to suppress her feelings or even change them to support her partner. She does need to express them in a way that doesn't make him feel attacked, accused, or blamed. Making a few small changes can make a big difference.

SEPTEMBER 16

How to Get a Man to Just Listen

*W*hen a woman says "You don't understand," she really means "You don't understand that right now I don't need a solution."

He hears that she doesn't appreciate his solution and then gets hooked into arguing about the validity of his approach and explaining himself at a time when she only needs to talk.

When a man is giving solutions and a woman just wants to talk, she needs to remind him of that while allowing him to save face. She could say something like, "That's a good idea. Let me just get this out and then we can discuss what to do." Then after she has talked for a while she can say, "Thanks so much for listening. I guess I just needed to get that out. Now I feel much better." Then she should simply walk away as if she has something to do.

SEPTEMBER 17

Communication, Intimacy, and Romance

*C*ommunication is essential for intimacy and romance to thrive, but timing is equally important. Lasting romance requires talking at the right time and in a way that doesn't offend, hurt, or sour your partner. When we have something difficult to communicate, we must choose our time wisely. Before sharing our discontent about something, we must make sure that some time has passed during which our partner was feeling loved and supported.

Having lots of successful romantic rituals gives men and women the emotional support they need to be more honest, particularly about the important things. When a man feels appreciated, it is easier for him to hear and respond lovingly to a woman's feelings and needs. When he doesn't feel appreciated and hears her talk about problems, he feels as if she is saying he is not doing enough.

Listening to a woman's feelings is a new skill for men. Traditionally, men have not been expected to listen to women's feelings. If a woman was upset, he would do something or fix something to make her feel better. When a woman needed empathy, she didn't talk to a man, she went to other women for emotional support. Until recently, women didn't even want to talk with men about their feelings.

As we learn this new skill, it opens the door to a greater intimacy between men and women than at any time in history. As men and women get closer through better communication, the possibility of lasting romance can become a common reality.

How Men Give Points

*W*hen a woman appreciates what a man does for her, he gets much of the love he needs. More than support, men primarily need appreciation. A man requires equal participation from a woman in doing the domestic duties of day-to-day life, but if he is not appreciated, her contribution is nearly meaningless and completely unimportant to him.

Similarly, a woman cannot appreciate the big things a man does for her unless he is also doing a lot of little things. Doing a lot of little things fulfills her primary needs to feel cared for, understood, and respected.

A major source of love for a man is the loving reaction that a woman has to his behavior. His love tank is not necessarily filled by what she does for him; it is mainly filled by how she reacts to him, or how she feels about him.

While men need to feel appreciated for their support, women need to feel supported.

A man needs to prioritize his loving behavior, for this will ensure that his partner's love needs are met. It will open her heart and open his. A man's heart opens as he succeeds in fulfilling a woman.

A woman needs to prioritize her loving attitudes and feelings, which will ensure that her partner's love needs are fulfilled. As a woman is able to express loving attitudes and feelings toward a man, he feels motivated to give more. This then assists her in opening her heart even more. A woman's heart opens more as she is able to get the support she needs.

SEPTEMBER 19

The Awakening of Our Inner Qualities

*W*hen men and women are attracted to each other, a tension is produced. The two, each independent, seek to fuse together. By getting closer through relating, being together, doing things together, communicating, sharing, touching, and sex, they release tension and experience bliss, happiness, peace, inspiration, freedom, confidence, and fulfillment.

These wonderful feelings are the result of awakening to our inner qualities, which in turn makes us feel whole. Unfortunately, this bliss is not lasting. It is but a glimpse of how we will feel when we are truly whole and balanced. To become whole, these potential qualities must begin to emerge into our conscious being.

To whatever extent we resist these emerging qualities, we will lose the pleasure and may even experience its opposite. By learning to love our partners at difficult and challenging times, we are opening the door to experience wholeness within ourselves.

SEPTEMBER 20

When Men Feel and Talk a Lot

Some men are already in touch with their feelings. They are very open and ready to talk. These men can unknowingly sabotage a relationship. A woman needs to feel first that a man is there for her; then she can be there for him without losing herself. When a man needs a woman more than she needs him, it can be a real turnoff. By making sure that he never talks more than the woman, a man creates the right balance in the relationship.

SEPTEMBER 21

The Autumn of Love

As a result of tending the garden during the summer, we get to harvest the results of our hard work. Fall has come. It is a golden time, rich and fulfilling. We experience a more mature love that accepts and understands our partner's imperfections as well as our own. It is a time of thanksgiving and sharing. Having worked hard during summer, we can relax and enjoy the love we have created.

How She Offends Him

*J*ust as well-intentioned men mistakenly try to "fix" women, women try to "improve" men at those times when a man talks about what is bothering him. All it takes is one or two objectionable comments, and he will fall silent. At such times, a woman generally has little idea of how she antagonized him. She doesn't realize that any attempt to help or improve him will be offensive.

This is a mistake that women commonly make, having no idea of how they offend the men in their lives. Men have a feminine side and from time to time need to share their thoughts and emotions to feel better. When this happens, a woman can easily shut a man down. All it takes is a few such experiences, and he will stop sharing what he needs to share.

SEPTEMBER 23

Why Talking Helps Romance

*T*oday, women don't have time for each other. To various degrees, they are all feeling overwhelmed with too much to do. Lacking the support of other women and having to talk in a very goal-oriented way at work, many women are not merely hungry to share their feelings at the end of the day but starving. This new dilemma can actually be a terrific opportunity for romance.

Men need to feel needed and appreciated. This is their primary emotional fuel. A big problem arises when women can provide for and protect themselves. In a very real way, men are out of work; they have been laid off from the job they have held exclusively for thousands of years.

Women have a new emerging need: a man to talk to, a partner who truly cares and listens. Women today need to communicate and feel heard at the end of the day. The new job for men is to provide the emotional support of listening to her at the end of the day. This kind of support creates a new intimacy between men and women, which lays the foundation for lasting attraction and passion.

SEPTEMBER 24

"You're Not Listening"

A common expression women use that is a complete turnoff for men is "You're not listening." When a woman uses this phrase, it frustrates a man because he usually is listening in some way, or at least trying to. Even if he wasn't, it is hard for him to hear it because in childhood it was used repeatedly by his mother when she was upset with him.

Hearing it in adulthood, a man feels as if his mate is talking down to him and treating him like a child. He hears it as not only degrading but also very controlling. He feels she is blaming him, when she is really just trying to be heard.

> *Just as a woman doesn't want to mother a man,*
> *a man does not want to be mothered.*

When a woman says, "You're not listening," it is generally because a man is not giving her his full attention. He is hearing her with only part of his mind when she wants his full attention. Instead she can say, "Would you give me your full attention?"

To a man, there is a world of difference between these two statements. He can't argue with the second message, but the first only pushes him farther away.

When a man is half-listening, distracted, or looking away while a woman is talking, she quite commonly communicates the message that he is not listening by raising her voice. Getting louder for a woman is another way of saying "You're not listening." The result is the same; in the end he will listen less. Yelling at children also programs them not to listen.

Negative critical feedback just doesn't work. For most women, the only other option is to get upset and walk away. Although her options seem bleak, there is hope. By using new communication skills, a woman can immediately begin getting the results she wants.

～～～

Men Need Solutions; Women Need to Share

*M*en instinctively look for solutions. When a man has a problem, the first thing he does is go to his cave and try to find a solution on his own. If he can find a solution or plan of action, he will feel better. If he doesn't find a solution, he will come out of his cave, find another man whom he respects, and talk about it.

When a man shares a problem with another man, he is generally looking for another opinion to help solve his problem. If he receives a good solution, he will immediately feel better. When a woman is upset and starts talking, a man assumes that she is looking for a solution to her problems. He has no reference point to let him know that she really just needs to be heard for a while. So he tries to help by solving her problems, which usually ends up invalidating and frustrating her.

**When a woman is upset, her first need
is for it to be okay to be upset for a while.**

She needs him to listen to her feelings without trying to fix her. By sharing her problems in a nonfocused way, she will naturally feel better. Her feeling of being overwhelmed will diminish even if all her problems remain unsolved.

When he understands this difference, a man can relax when a woman is sharing. Instead of feeling responsible for solving all her problems, he can simply focus on solving one problem: he can fulfill her need for a fully focused listener, which will help her to feel better.

SEPTEMBER 26

Why We Argue

Men and women commonly argue about money, sex, decisions, scheduling, values, child rearing, and household responsibilities. These discussions and negotiations turn into painful arguments for only one reason: we are not feeling loved. Emotional pain comes from not feeling loved, and when a person is feeling emotional pain, it is hard to be loving.

Because women are not from Mars, they do not instinctively realize what a man needs in order to deal successfully with disagreements. Conflicting ideas, feelings, and desires are a difficult challenge for a man. The closer he is to a woman, the harder it is to deal with differences and disagreements. When she doesn't like something he has done, he tends to take it very personally and feels she doesn't like him.

We are never arguing for the reasons we think.

A man can handle differences and disagreements best when his emotional needs are being fulfilled. When he is deprived of the love he needs, he becomes defensive and his dark side begins to emerge. Instinctively he draws his sword. On the surface he may seem to be arguing about the issue (money, responsibilities, and so forth), but the real reason he has drawn his sword is that he doesn't feel loved.

Though all these painful feelings and needs are valid, they are generally not dealt with and communicated directly. Instead, they build up inside and come bursting forth during an argument. Sometimes they are directly addressed, but usually they surface and are expressed through facial expression, body posture, and tone of voice.

Men and women need to understand and cooperate with their particular sensitivities and not resent them. You will be addressing the true problem by trying to communicate in a way that fulfills your partner's emotional needs. Arguments can then become mutually supportive conversations necessary to resolve and negotiate differences and disagreements.

The Importance of Eye Contact

*W*hen women are upset, they want to be seen. Unlike men, they don't want to be ignored or left alone. The most important thing a man can do is to notice when his partner is upset. When she feels seen, she can more directly see herself and more efficiently explore her feelings.

When a man listens, his basic tendency is to look away in order to think about what is being said. It is hard for women to understand this difference because when they talk about their feelings with each other, they deliver their support by lots of eye contact.

If a man simply stares into a woman's eyes when she talks about feelings, his mind will start to go blank and he will space out. Without understanding that a woman needs more eye contact than he does, a man tends to look away to figure out what his partner means or how he is going to respond.

When a man sustains eye contact, he tends to space out.

Learning to maintain eye contact not only delivers a very important kind of support but also helps a man restrain his tendency to offer a solution to her problems. The trick for a man is not only to remember to do it, but also to do it without going blank.

This can be accomplished if he looks in a special way. Instead of staring, he should first look into her eyes for two to three seconds. Then, when he would naturally turn his head and look away, he should instead look to the tip of her nose. After that, he should look at her lips, then her chin, and then her whole face. Then he should start over.

This procedure keeps him looking in her direction, yet frees him from spacing out or going blank. It can also be relaxing because it is something else he can do instead of passively doing nothing.

SEPTEMBER 28

How Men Go Out of Balance

*M*en in relationships will at first be objective and then become subjective. This means that in the beginning of a relationship a man tries to improve things by making his partner happy when she appears unhappy. His instinctive strategy is to change the object: if she is unhappy, he tries to make her happy by fulfilling her needs.

**Men are most positive when
they maintain an objective attitude.**

If he begins to feel that he can't make a difference, he goes out of balance, becomes overly subjective, and his attitude changes. He may feel self-righteous, defiant, resentful, spiteful, punitive, unforgiving, and judgmental. As a result he becomes weak, moody, insecure, and passive. He loses his confidence and is no longer willing to take risks. He may even develop negative patterns for getting his way through emotional outbursts and tantrums. It is hard for him to shake off his negative mood when he has lost his objectivity.

A man, being objective by nature, can best change himself by recognizing and solving problems outside himself. For example, a man becomes more loving and sensitive by recognizing how others are hurt or affected by certain things he does or does not do. With greater insight into how he can solve a problem, a man is suddenly free from the grip of negative attitudes. He automatically becomes more willing to adjust his behavior to solve the problem. By solving the problem, he begins to feel his positive feelings again.

SEPTEMBER 29

How a Woman Changes

*T*o cope with stress, a woman can change herself in a very natural way. In a sense she is really not changing but becoming more of who she already is. Being subjective by nature, she changes herself by sharing and expressing her feelings, thoughts, and wishes without being invalidated. To do this, she needs to be heard with caring, understanding, and respect. These very important aspects of love nurture her and help to center her.

If she keeps her feelings to herself, she will gradually lose touch with who she is. Her thinking will become shallow, superficial, and rigid. She will not be able to adapt lovingly and gracefully to the stresses of life, work, and relationships. She will be consumed by trying to adjust her behavior and speech to win the love of others. From this place of seeking to earn love, she will try to change others to get the love she needs. At this point she loses her ability to adapt and change in response to stress. She is unable to sustain a truly loving and positive attitude.

At times of stress, it is easy for a woman with low self-esteem to adjust her behavior and speech in relating to others. It is much more difficult to change or transform her feelings. She may give the appearance of a loving and giving person, but deep inside she is hiding a storehouse of resentment, mistrust, and dissatisfaction. These negative feelings weaken her identity and her relationships.

With this new insight into how she can nurture and transform her negative feelings through communication or talk therapy, once again she can free herself from this self-destructive pattern and experience her loving self.

Disagree with Him, but Don't Disapprove of Him

*M*ost painful arguments occur not because two people disagree but because either the man feels that the woman disapproves of his point of view or the woman disapproves of the way he is talking to her. She often may disapprove of him because he is not validating her point of view or not speaking to her in a caring way. When men and women learn to approve and validate, they don't have to argue. They can discuss and negotiate differences.

Just as women need validation, men need approval. The more a man loves a woman, the more he needs her approval. It is always there in the beginning of a relationship. Either she gives him the message that she approves of him or he feels confident that he can win her approval. In either case, the approval is present.

Women are generally oblivious to the way they withdraw their approval. When they do withdraw it, they feel very justified in doing so. A reason for this insensitivity is that women are unaware of how significant approval is for men.

> **When a woman withdraws her approval,**
> **it is particularly painful to a man.**

A woman can learn to disagree with a man's behavior and still approve of who he is. For a man to feel loved, he needs her to approve of who he is even if she disagrees with his behavior. Generally, when a woman disagrees with a man's behavior and wants to change him, she will disapprove of him. Certainly there may be times when she is more approving or less approving of him, but to be disapproving is very painful and hurts him.

Most men are too embarrassed to admit how much they need approval. They may go to great lengths to prove they don't care. But why do they immediately become cold, distant, and defensive when they lose a woman's approval? Because not getting what they really need hurts.

A man can deal with a woman's disappointment, but when it is expressed with disapproval or rejection, he feels wounded by her. Women commonly interrogate a man about his behavior with a disapproving tone. They do this because they think it will teach him a lesson. It does not. It only creates fear and resentment. Gradually he becomes less and less motivated to change.

To approve of a man is to see the good reasons behind what he does. Even when he is irresponsible or lazy or disrespectful, a woman can find and recognize the goodness within him if she loves him. To approve is to find the loving intention or the goodness behind the external behavior.

❧ OCTOBER ❧

Attract, Flirt, Respect

*A*ttraction, flirtation, and respect are three complex actions that either bring us together or pull us apart.

Attraction is not under our control. We can be sure that when there is attraction, there are lessons to learn and discoveries to be made. Since we are attracted to people who are unlike ourselves, the fundamental basis for enriching relationships is the acknowledgment that people are different.

A woman's flirting responses to a man's pursuit are very exciting because a man is always looking for the opportunity to take credit for a woman's happiness. It compliments his ability to make a woman happy. Being successful in the pursuit is as much fun for him as it is for a woman to feel that someone she likes is trying to make her happy.

Finally, respect for one's partner means supporting them in being themselves, upholding their individuality. Respect honors another's needs, wishes, values, and rights. To respect is to keep agreements and honor commitments. It is to give equal and sometimes greater importance to another. Respect recognizes that a person deserves support without having to earn it.

Although we cannot control attraction, we can make sure we do what is required to sustain it. To keep the magic of love and attraction alive, we must actively create opportunites for romance as well as continue to meet our partner's emotional needs. To create romance, women must remember to flirt actively with their partners, while men must continue the pursuit. To fuel this occasional romance, we must remember to honor and nurture our partner daily.

The True Challenge of Love

*W*e are drawn to that which is different. Our challenge is to understand, accept, and appreciate those differences, and then they will naturally emerge within ourselves.

This is a challenge because the process is not always easy. Intense attraction to someone is a sign that there are many differences to harmonize, many conflicts to resolve. Attraction is not under our control. We can be sure that when there is attraction, there are lessons to be learned and discoveries to be made. Because we are attracted to people who are unlike ourselves, the fundamental basis for enriching relationships is the acknowledgment that people are different.

OCTOBER 2

Attraction

*A*lthough feelings of attraction are automatic, in order to sustain attraction in a personal relationship we must be skillful in presenting ourselves in ways that are not just appealing to the other sex but supportive as well. It is not enough to say, "Here I am; take me as I am." The alchemy of creating a loving relationship is a delicate balance of give-and-take.

Quite often it is the anticipation that we can get what we need or want from a relationship that tends to sustain attraction. Without a clear message that we can get what we need, that attraction will disappear. It can be so easy to misinterpret our date's actions and reactions and be turned off simply because we think and feel so differently. One of the biggest challenges in the beginning of a relationship is to sustain the feeling of attraction and give it a chance to grow as we get to know someone.

Women and Physical Attraction

By exercising her discernment and choosing to date only men to whom she feels both mentally and emotionally attracted, a woman begins to discover her physical attraction for a partner. She wants not just to be touched by his mind and heart but to be touched physically. At this level, when a man holds her hand, puts his arm around her, or gives her a kiss, a lot of physical attraction is felt.

When a woman already feels mental and emotional chemistry, she will begin to feel physical attraction. Only a few men at this stage will provide all three levels of chemistry. Many men may seem attractive to her, but only a few will stimulate her mentally and emotionally. By holding to this standard in her relationships, she gives her discernment a chance to grow.

~≈≈~

Men Feel Physical Attraction First

*W*hen a man meets his soul mate, there is almost always a spark of physical attraction to start with. When it is not there, it could simply be that he doesn't understand the importance of having standards. He simply follows his attractions and doesn't learn to become more discerning about his choices. A man temporarily loses his ability to feel physical attraction for a woman who could possibly be his soul mate when he consciously chooses to pursue other women he clearly knows are not his type.

The more a man pursues women he could not love, the less he is able to feel physically attracted to a woman he could love. By learning from his experience to distinguish between the women to whom he is attracted, a man gets closer to finding the right person for him.

This physical attraction is the first and lowest level of discernment for men. Generally, a young man starts out on this level. Even a more mature man may regress to this level when he is on the rebound from a relationship. A hungry man is not picky about what food he eats.

Though physical attraction is the foundation for a man's discernment to build on, it is still mindless. A woman needs to remember that even if a man does not know anything about her except how she looks, he will suddenly start to feel physically attracted. His attraction has nothing to do with who this woman is, nor does it reflect a willingness or desire to know her or have a relationship with her. He only wants to see more, touch more, and feel more.

OCTOBER 5

How Men Unnecessarily Feel Rejected

*M*any times a woman is potentially in the mood for sex but a man just doesn't realize it. He ends up feeling rejected when she might really want to have sex.

Sometimes a man will ask her any of the following questions:

"Would you like to have sex?"

"Do you want to have sex?"

"Are you in the mood for sex?"

If she responds "I'm not sure" or "I don't know" to any of these questions, he will generally misunderstand and mistakenly hear rejection. He thinks she is politely saying no when she is really saying she doesn't know. This is hard for men to understand. When a man is asked if he wants sex, he has a definite response. He generally knows for certain if he wants to have sex.

When a woman is unsure about wanting sex, it means that she needs a little time, attention, and talking to find out. With this new awareness, a man can easily overcome his tendency to feel rejected immediately and give up his pursuit.

꩜

What to Expect in a Relationship

*W*hen approached in the right way and at the right time, men are happy to do more. With a few months of good communication, no demands, and several doses of appreciation, any man will be willing to do more. But a man's idea of more may be dramatically different from a woman's.

It is unrealistic to expect a man suddenly to be motivated to do fifty percent of the housework if he has been used to doing much less. Likewise, if he is the quiet type, it is not probable that he will immediately open up and share his feelings.

As women begin to accept the fact that they can ask for and get more without having to nag or complain, they give up their resistance to giving a man the daily appreciation he requires. They assume full responsibility for communicating needs, confident that they can get them fulfilled. They don't expect men to know what they need instinctively, but patiently and persistently appreciate what men do give and gradually ask for more.

꣠꣠

Adjusting Our Expectations

*J*ust as a woman needs to adjust the expectation that a man will listen to her feelings and share all domestic duties, so a man must adjust his expectation that a woman will speak in a loving, pleasing manner, make no demands of him, and be fulfilled when he gets home. In essence, women need to release the expectation that men will do everything they want, and men need to release the expectation that women will always be loving and happy.

Through practicing his new relationship skills, instead of feeling annoyed by a woman's feelings of discontent, a man can begin to see them as opportunities to make her happier. When a woman is not getting the support she wants, she can see it as an opportunity to take responsibility for getting what she needs. She can view it as an opportunity to practice expressing greater power, but in a feminine way. This is generally something her mother could not tell her.

When a woman is unhappy and talks about problems, a man doesn't have to feel blamed. He can reverse this pattern by understanding her real need to share. When she claims to feel a lack in the relationship, he realizes that it is not because of his deficiency, although it may always sound that way, but because our modern culture doesn't sufficiently support her feminine side. This frees him to consider her feelings rather than defend himself. It also greatly clarifies what he is required to do.

When a woman is disappointed by her partner, instead of taking it personally, she can reverse the pattern and recognize his loving intent and willingness to support her more but in small steps. By adjusting her expectations, she can eventually connect with the grace of her feminine spirit, which does not demand perfection but seeks to love and embrace life just the way it is. She realizes that it is not personal but that he was not trained by his father's example in how to fulfill a modern woman's new needs.

OCTOBER 8

Living in the Promise

*Q*uite commonly, a woman makes the mistake of anticipating what a man will give her if she is loving to him. In a sense, she lives in the promise of getting his love, and so she becomes more loving.

When a woman lives in the promise of a man's love because she believes that she will get what she needs, she is happy to give in advance. The more she gives in advance, the happier she becomes because she assumes she will get it all in return.

When a woman gives in advance and not in response to what a man gives, it can have the effect of making him less interested.

It is a mistake to believe that if she turns him on, fulfills his every need, and happily accommodates his wishes, he will do the same for her. Some women are taught that for a woman to get a man to love her, she should be pleased by everything he does, wait on him hand and foot, and laugh at all his jokes. Although this might work if he did this for her, when a woman gives in this way, she unknowingly lessens the attraction.

Men can also live in the promise. A man can fall in love with a woman and feel that he is the right man for her, that he holds the key to her ultimate happiness. Because he anticipates making her so happy, he behaves as if she is perfect. He behaves as if he is certain that he can make her happy. When a man's behavior is too strong and he promises too much too quickly, it can backfire and cause a woman to close up.

By taking the time to move together through the five stages of dating and by staying in touch with current feelings after marriage, both men and women can minimize the illusion of living in the promise.

~~~※~~~

Women and Soul Attraction

As a result of her growing discernment, a woman eventually develops her ability to experience soul attraction. She is able to fall in love with a man who has stimulated her on all four levels of attraction. She reaches level four, soul attraction, when her heart is open. She will begin to see many men as lovable, but not necessarily the one for her.

To various degrees, she could love these men, but she gradually learns to recognize which of these men is the perfect soul mate for her. Her open heart makes her capable of eventually seeing the good in her partner, even though he is neither perfect nor able to fulfill all her needs.

As her love grows, she is able to discern whether he is right for her, not because of his ability to be the perfect partner but because in herself she feels an unconditional love that recognizes "This is the person I am here to be with." This realization is not something she has concluded on the basis of comparisons of what is available or what could be possible. Her soul just knows.

While the couple will still experience the normal challenges that any two people would experience, there is a deep soul connection they keep coming back to that helps them overcome the inevitable conflicts, frustrations, and disappointments of any relationship.

❧

How to Attract Mr. Right

*V*ery independent and self-sufficient women in their thirties and forties often ask me how to attract a man.

My response is to ask them why they *need* a man. The question invariably takes them by surprise. They give such answers as "Well, I don't know if I really *need* a man" or "I don't really *need* a man, but I want one."

If these women are to secure a lasting relationship, they must first begin to open up to their feminine side, which feels no shame in saying "I need a man."

Though needing a man will attract him, being needy or desperate is a turnoff. When a woman is in a hurry for a relationship, she is definitely feeling from her female side, but she is too needy to attract the right man.

> *It is difficult to discern the difference between needing and being needy, so many women deny their needs altogether.*

By first taking some time to nurture her female side without depending on a man, something magical begins to happen. She feels her need for a man and trusts that at the right time and in the right place she will find him. This openness can be cultivated by finding fulfillment in her female friendships without depending on a man yet remaining open to receiving a man's support.

OCTOBER 11

❧

How Men Experience Intimacy

*W*e must always keep in mind that a man bonds emotionally by successfully doing for a woman. A man experiences greater intimacy each time he succeeds in providing his partner with fulfillment. We must remember that women experience greater intimacy primarily by receiving love and support. This is a very important distinction. If a woman cannot slow down and allow a man to nurture her female side, she will have trouble creating a bond in the first place.

A simple example of the new relationship skill of slowing down can be seen simply and graphically: a man and woman approach a door. Women who do too much will speed up, politely open the door, and wait for the man to walk through. They give to others what they need themselves, which only reinforces the tendency to give and not receive.

To nurture her female side, a woman should practice slowing down to make sure he gets to the door first, waiting for him to open it, walking through, and then thanking him. When she lets him open the door for her, she gives him an opportunity to support her successfully.

Why Very Attractive Women Get Very Annoyed

*T*he more physically attractive a woman is, the more annoyed she may become with men. Men who have no deep interest in her are constantly pursuing her. Although she may at first feel flattered by their attentions, after a series of disappointments, they can become a source of resentment.

These women have a right to be upset. They innocently responded to a man's advances and then felt disappointed or betrayed when he was not interested in pursuing a relationship. They felt in some way tricked by his sudden shift in interest. What these women don't realize is how they are a part of the problem because they do not realize how men and women are different.

A man can want to have sex without yet knowing if he wants a relationship. In this he is different from most women. When a woman feels a strong desire to have sex, she also feels a desire to have a relationship with a man. When he wants sex, she mistakenly assumes that he also wants a relationship. But many men decide if they want to have a relationship only after sex.

Even though the sex was great, he may decide not to pursue a relationship. Without an understanding of this difference, women can assume that they were being tricked and taken advantage of.

To make sure she doesn't feel hurt, a woman must make sure that she is not expecting more from a man after having sex. If they don't have a relationship, it is unrealistic for her to expect one just because she was a willing sexual partner.

OCTOBER 13

Friendship, Autonomy, and Fun

*F*riendship is a breeze if we suppress our feelings. If one partner is willing to sacrifice who they are to the relationship, they will always get along—but the passion will die.

Make no mistake: although women quite commonly lose themselves to accommodate their partner, men also surrender a major part of themselves. To avoid conflict, a man will hold himself back. Without good communication skills, a couple with a lot of love may often choose to maintain their friendship and sacrifice their feelings. They do not realize that by suppressing negative feelings they are also suppressing their ability to feel in general.

When a woman cares for a man but doesn't ask for what she wants, she is actually hurting, not helping, the relationship. A man can thrive in a relationship only when he truly fulfills her needs. If she pretends to be fulfilled, he will think he is fulfilled, but he doesn't even know what he is missing.

> *A man can thrive in a relationship only*
> *when he truly fulfills his partner's needs.*

To be really good friends in a relationship requires a balance of autonomy and dependence. Needing our partners is the basis of passion. If we are not also autonomous, at those times when our partners have little to give us we will feel powerless to get what we need and fall into blaming them.

By practicing personal responsibility and self-healing, we can nurture ourselves at those times when our partners can't. The real test of love is when we can be our partner's friend and give without demanding anything in return. This becomes easier when we have repeatedly experienced that they can be there for us. When we are confident that we can get what we need at other times, we are not so demanding at those times when our partners have little to give.

❧❧

Women Love Great Sex

Great sex requires a positive attitude about sex. For a man to continue feeling attracted to his partner, he needs to feel that she likes sex as much as he does. Quite often a man will feel defeated in sex because he mistakenly gets the message that his partner is not as interested in sex as he is. Without a deeper understanding of how we are wired differently for sex, it is very easy to feel discouraged.

Women love great sex as much as men do. The difference between a woman and a man is that she doesn't feel a strong desire for sex unless her need for love is first satisfied. Most important, she first needs to feel loved and special to a man. When her heart is opened in this way, her sexual center begins to open and she feels a longing as great as or greater than any man feels. To her, love is much more important than sex, but as the need for love is fulfilled, the importance of sex dramatically increases.

How to Initiate a Conversation with a Man

*T*he more a woman tries to get a man to talk, the more he will resist. Directly trying to get him to talk is not the best approach, especially if he is stretching away. Instead of wondering how she can get him to talk, she might consider, "How can I achieve greater intimacy, conversation, and communication with my partner?"

If a woman feels the need for more talk in the relationship, and most women do, she can initiate more conversation but with a mature awareness that not only accepts but also expects that sometimes he will be available and at other times he will instinctively pull away.

When he is available, instead of asking him twenty questions or demanding that he talk, she can let him know that she appreciates him even if he just listens. In the beginning, she should even discourage him from talking. This nondemanding approach encourages a man to listen more.

Without appreciation and encouragement, a man may lose interest because he feels as though his listening is "doing nothing." He doesn't realize how valuable his listening is to a woman. Most women instinctively know how important listening is. To expect a man to know this without some training is to expect him to be like a woman. Fortunately, after being appreciated for listening to a woman, a man does learn to respect the value of talking.

❧❧

Men Pursue and Women Flirt

To create a relationship, a woman must be careful not to pursue a man but instead be responsive to his pursuit. This kind of receptiveness and responsiveness is expressed through flirting. When a woman flirts with a man, she is simply interacting in a manner that expresses the feeling that maybe he could be the man to make her happy, maybe he could be that great guy she has been looking for her whole life, maybe he could be capable of fulfilling her needs, maybe he could be the one she wants to share a really special time with, or maybe he could just be interesting or fun.

Flirting is like shopping. When a woman shops, she has fun checking out what she likes and does not like. Flirting energy says, "I am looking and liking what I see. Maybe you could be the one to make me happy."

A woman's flirting responses to a man's pursuit are very exciting because a man is always looking for the opportunity to take credit for a woman's happiness. It validates his ability to make a woman happy.

~~~~~~~~

"Men Want Only One Thing"

*W*omen commonly think men want only one thing: sex. The truth is that men really want love. A man wants love just as much as a woman does, but before he can open his heart and let in his partner's love, sexual arousal is a prerequisite. Just as a woman needs love to open up to sex, a man needs sex to open up to love.

As a general guideline, a woman needs to be emotionally fulfilled before she can long for sexual contact. A man gets much of his emotional fulfillment during sex.

Women do not understand this about men. The hidden reason a man is so much in a hurry to have sex is that he is able to feel again through sex. Throughout the day, a man becomes so focused on his work that he loses touch with his loving feelings. Sex helps him to feel again. With sex, a man's heart begins to open up. With sex, a man can give and receive love.

When a woman begins to understand this difference, it changes her whole perspective on sex. Instead of seeing a man's desire for sex as something crude and divorced from love, she can begin to see it as his way of eventually finding love. A woman's feelings about a man's preoccupation with sex can dramatically shift when she understands why a man needs sex.

OCTOBER 18

꧁꧂

When a Woman Opens Her Heart

A man should not be discouraged if a woman is not immediately interested in him in a physical way. He needs to remember that a woman is like an oven that slowly warms up. If she just wants to be friends at first, it doesn't mean that he doesn't stand a chance. Quite often women who have found their soul mates say that at first they were just friends and that the romance came later. Their husbands almost always say that the physical attraction was there on their side from the beginning.

OCTOBER 19

꧁꧂

When Love Fails

*L*ove often fails because people instinctively give what they want. Because a woman's primary love needs are to be cared for and understood, she automatically gives her man a lot of caring and understanding. To a man this caring support often feels as though she doesn't trust him. Being trusted is his primary need, not being cared for.

When he doesn't respond positively to her caring, she can't understand why he doesn't appreciate her brand of support. He, of course, is giving his own brand of love, which isn't what she needs. So they are caught in a loop of failing to fulfill each other's needs.

Many people give up when relationships become too difficult. Relationships become easier when we understand our partner's primary needs. Without giving more but by giving what is required, we do not burn out. This understanding of the different kinds of love finally explains why our sincere attempts to love fail. To fulfill your partner, you need to learn how to give the love they primarily need.

OCTOBER 20

Men Who Talk Too Much

*T*he most effective way to get a man's full attention is to prepare him for the conversation by letting him off the hook of needing to talk more. By letting him know in advance that he doesn't have to talk, you allow him to relax and listen instead of figuring out what to say. After all, you are the one who wants to talk.

This is a very important awareness. A man can be out of the cave and be open to conversation but not have anything to say. Instinctively he doesn't feel the need to initiate conversation. When a woman senses that he doesn't have anything to say, she feels awkward talking more and asking him to listen.

It feels rude to her to say something like "Well, even if you don't feel like talking, I have a lot to say. Would you listen to me? You don't have to say anything." She doesn't know that to him this is not rudeness. It is directness, and it is not demanding. Men love this kind of support.

By being prepared in this way, a man doesn't need to resist the listening process because it has been clearly stated that he doesn't have to say anything.

OCTOBER 21

The Female Need to Be Respected

*A*s one shares in a relationship, it is essential to maintain one's sense of self. Respecting one's partner means not trying to change or manipulate them but rather supporting them in being themselves and upholding their rights. Respect honors another's needs, wishes, values, and rights. To respect is to keep agreements and honor commitments. It is to give equal importance and sometimes greater importance to another.

The need to be respected is the need to be yourself in a relationship without giving up who you are. When a person feels respected they don't feel that they have to earn their rights; they don't feel unworthy. The need for respect is the need for fairness as well as the acknowledgment that you are entitled. Respect recognizes that a person deserves support without having to earn it.

OCTOBER 22

Opening Our Hearts

*I*f we feel we are not getting the love we need and are blaming our partner, it is a clear sign that we need something our partner cannot presently give us.

Taking responsibility for supporting ourselves when our hearts are closed frees us from dwelling on our partner as the problem and allows us to examine the situation on a much more fundamental level. We are able to nurture ourselves and then come back to the relationship with more to give, not more to demand.

Blame is always off the track.

Instead of drowning in negativity and reacting in unloving ways when our hearts are closed, we can use this "downtime" for self-healing. Instead of looking to our partner to change when we are blaming them, we should focus on changing ourselves. When we are feeling open and forgiving, we can refocus and look for ways to solve or correct the problem that originally upset us.

OCTOBER 23

Setting and Respecting Limits

A woman needs to recognize the boundaries of what she can give without resenting her partner. Instead of expecting her partner to even the score, she needs to keep it even by regulating how much she gives. She must pace herself like a long-distance runner so that she doesn't run out of energy too soon.

It is okay and even healthy
to hold back from giving sometimes.

As a man experiences limits, he is motivated to give more. By respecting limits, he is automatically motivated to question the effectiveness of his behavior patterns and to start making changes. When a woman realizes that in order to receive she needs to set limits, she begins to forgive her partner and explore new ways of asking for and receiving support. When a woman sets limits, she gradually learns to relax and receive more.

OCTOBER 24

What Makes a Woman Special

A woman first feels that she is special to a man when he feels physically attracted to her. A woman must remember that she is not that special, because there are a lot of women to whom a man can feel physically attracted. It is a good beginning, but it doesn't necessarily mean anything more. To him, in that moment, she may be the ultimate woman of his dreams. In this case, he may believe and behave as though he were in love with who she is, but only time will tell, by giving him an opportunity to get to know her.

A woman becomes more special to a man when he finds that not only is he physically attracted to her, but he also likes her. There are many women to whom he can be physically attracted, but only a smaller group with whom he can also be friends. A woman becomes even more special to him when he finds that he is mentally attracted to her. There are only a few women for whom he can feel all three levels of chemistry.

She becomes still more special when he is able to see her as an imperfect person who is lovable. Even during difficult times with her, he is able to see the good in her and feel his love for her. This kind of unconditional love makes her very special. Within this very small and special group, his soul picks one to share his life. It is then that a woman is most special to a man.

OCTOBER 25

The Power of Touch

A man reaching out to touch or hold hands is a turn-on for a woman. Men generally hold hands in the courting stage, but they stop after a while. This is a big loss. A woman loves to feel that a man wants to connect with her in this way. She doesn't feel loved if the only time he wants to touch her is when he wants sex.

If a man wants his partner to feel receptive to sex, he needs to touch her in an affectionate way many times each day when he is not wanting sex. He can hold hands, put his arm around her, stroke her shoulders and arms, all without implying that he is wanting sex. If the only time he touches her is when he wants sex, she begins to feel used or taken for granted.

A woman needs to be touched in a variety of ways many times a day.

When he is holding her hand, he should remember to be attentive. Many times a man will forget what he is doing and she is left holding a limp, lifeless hand. When he needs to shift his attention, he should just release her hand. She doesn't want to hold hands all the time. It is just a way to connect for a few minutes.

Not only is touching her a great way to connect and feel close, but it also softens the rough edges at difficult times and brings us back to feeling our love for each other.

OCTOBER 26

Men Love a Woman with a Smile

*T*he secret to attracting a man is an attitude of gratitude. When a woman is appreciative of the blessings in her life, she becomes increasingly more attractive. When she takes time to give thanks for the fullness in her life, it gives a man confidence that he can succeed in making her happy. Taking a little time each day to give thanks not only motivates her partner to give more but also helps with her true self.

OCTOBER 27

Emotional Attraction

*E*motional chemistry has a lot to do with personality. Personality is how you relate to the world and others. Quite often opposite personalities are attracted to each other. For example, some men like a woman with a bubbly or perky personality, while others like a more stable or relaxed personality. The possibilities are endless. We can be attracted to someone like ourselves, but generally we are most attracted to people who are not like ourselves.

A very stable personality with somewhat fixed routines may be attracted to a person who likes change and excitement. A very bold, outwardly directed personality may be attracted to a shy, inwardly directed person. A very assertive personality may be attracted to a more supportive or accommodating personality. An easygoing personality may be attracted to a more formal personality.

A playful personality is not intrinsically more attractive than any other. It is how someone complements who we are that determines the chemistry we feel. As we become more discerning, we find that we are automatically attracted to the people we could be friends with.

OCTOBER 28

Remembering Our Differences

*B*oth men and women can benefit greatly by remembering how differently we keep score. Improving a relationship takes no more energy than we are already expending and doesn't have to be terribly difficult. Relationships are exhausting until we learn how to direct our energies in ways our partner can fully appreciate.

OCTOBER 29

Temptation

*E*very time a man is tempted by the possibility of sex and maintains his monogamous commitment, he is creating the safety for his partner to enjoy sex more. By not indulging in his fantasies of other women, he learns to control his sexual energies so that he can slow down the process of release and last longer for her. Certainly thoughts and images may cross his mind, but as long as he comes back to an awareness of his partner, his passion and control will continue to grow.

OCTOBER 30

Love, Romance, and Monogamy

*B*y taking responsibility for our reactions and actions in a relationship, we can truly begin to give and receive love successfully. Without an awareness of how our partners specifically need love, we may be missing priceless opportunities.

Women primarily feel loved when they are receiving from their men the emotional and physical support they need. It does not matter so much what he provides as that he does it in a continuous way. A woman feels loved when she feels that a man's love is consistent.

When a man doesn't understand a woman, he tends to focus on the big ways to fulfill her all at once but will then ignore her for weeks. Good communication provides a healthy basis for a loving relationship. Romance is the dessert.

OCTOBER 31

Wise Men and Women

*M*en generally don't realize how their rubber-band behavior—suddenly pulling away and then returning—affects women. With this new insight about how women react to his intimacy cycle, a man can recognize the importance of sincerely listening when a woman speaks. He understands her and he does care. When-ever he is not needing to pull away, the wise man takes the time to initiate conversation by asking his female partner how she is feeling.

He grows to understand his own cycles and reassures her when he pulls away that he will be back. He might say, "I need some time to be alone, and then we will have some special time together with no distractions." Or if he starts to pull away while she is talking, he might say, "I need some time to think about this, and then we can talk again."

When he returns to talk, she might probe him to understand why he left. If he's not sure, which is many times the case, he might say, "I'm not sure. I just needed some time to myself. But let's continue our conversation."

To initiate a conversation, the wise woman learns not to demand that a man talk but asks that he just listen to her. As her emphasis changes, the pressure on him is released. She learns to open up and share her feelings without demanding that he do the same.

She trusts that he will gradually open up more as he feels accepted and listens to her feelings. She does not punish him or chase after him. She understands that sometimes her intimate feelings trigger his need to pull away, while at other times, when he is on his way back, he is quite capable of hearing her intimate feelings. This wise woman does not give up. She patiently and lovingly persists with a knowledge that few women have.

❧ NOVEMBER ❧

Trust, Happiness, Forgiveness

*T*he need to be trusted is the need for an acknowledgment from your partner that you are a good person. When trust is absent, people consistently jump to the wrong, negative conclusion regarding a person's intent, whereas trust gives every offense the benefit of the doubt. Trust grows in a relationship when each partner recognizes that the other does not intend to hurt, but seeks only to support.

A woman's trust in a man draws him to her. When a woman trusts a man, she is able to draw out the best in him. Of course, if she trusts him to be perfect, he will let her down. But if she trusts that he can and will help, he gets the message that he is of value and that his best is enough for her to accept and appreciate. Her trust will draw out of him increasing greatness.

It is hard to imagine happiness lasting in a relationship

without trust or the ability to forgive. In fact, to open our hearts to each other and enjoy a lifetime of love, the most important skill of all is forgiveness. Forgiving your partner for their mistakes not only frees you to love again but also allows you to forgive yourself for not being perfect. Forgiving, after all, means letting go of hurt.

One part of a woman that a man finds difficult to understand is her need to be supported in being unhappy. Without that support, she can never be truly happy. To be genuinely happy requires occasionally dipping down into the well to release, heal, and purify the emotions. This is a natural and healthy process.

Trust in the wonder of that process and give thanks for the many opportunities to grow together in love.

She Needs Reassurance, and He Needs Encouragement

*W*hen a man repeatedly shows that he cares, understands, respects, validates, and is devoted to his partner, her primary need to be reassured is fulfilled.

> **A reassuring attitude tells a woman**
> **that she is continually loved.**

A man commonly makes the mistake of thinking that once he has met all of a woman's primary love needs and she feels happy and secure, she should know from then on that she is loved. This is not the case. To fulfill her need to be loved, he must remember to reassure her again and again.

Similarly, a man needs to be encouraged by a woman. A woman's encouraging attitude gives hope and strength to a man by expressing confidence in his abilities and character. When a woman's attitude expresses trust, acceptance, appreciation, admiration, and approval, she encourages a man to be all that he can be. Feeling encouraged motivates him to give her the loving reassurance that she needs.

Male Forgetfulness

*F*ocus is necessary to get a job done, but it's possible to have too much. When masculine energy isn't balanced with feminine energy, it tends to focus on one thing to the exclusion of everything else. In the pursuit of one objective, nothing else gets done. This pattern is especially troublesome in relationships.

For instance, even though a man may love his wife very much, if his masculine and feminine sides are out of balance, he may forget important dates like their anniversary or her birthday, or simple things like picking something up at the store or taking phone messages. It is not that he doesn't care, but his awareness is focused in another direction.

> **By understanding why a man forgets,
> a woman finds it easier to be forgiving and accepting.**

This forgetfulness is hard for women to accept. A woman assumes that forgetfulness connotes lack of caring or interest. It's hard for her to believe that a man who forgets birthdays and anniversaries could really love her. After all, this kind of behavior is so foreign to her experience of loving someone. Men prioritize in the context of achieving their goals, while women prioritize according to the importance of their relationships. With this perspective, it is easy to see how men can unintentionally hurt the feelings of women.

NOVEMBER 3

She Needs Caring, and He Needs Trust

*W*hen a man shows interest in a woman's feelings and heartfelt concern for her well-being, she feels loved and cared for. When he makes her feel special in this caring way, he succeeds in fulfilling her primary need to feel as if someone cares about her. Naturally she begins to trust him more. When she trusts, she becomes more open and receptive.

When a woman's attitude is open and receptive toward a man, he feels trusted. To trust a man is to believe that he is doing his best and that he wants the best for his partner. When a woman's reactions reveal a positive belief in her man's abilities and intentions, his primary love need is fulfilled. Automatically, he is more caring and attentive to her feelings and needs.

When a Man Makes a Mistake

*D*uring a stressful situation, a man needs time to mull over his thoughts and feelings until he is able to understand what he did and how he could have done it differently. Then he will feel comfortable talking about what happened and why it happened. At this stage, he becomes more accountable for his mistakes. He can then change himself without feeling weak and submissive.

It is as though a man cannot admit he erred unless he can figure out a way he could have acted differently. He can recognize that he made a mistake when he realizes, "If I had known then what I now know, I could have and would have done things differently."

Partnership and Service to a Higher Purpose

*W*e all come into this world with gifts to share and purposes to fulfill beyond our personal happiness. They may not be earth-shattering, but they are there. For a relationship to grow in love and passion, the love we share with another needs to be directed in some loftier way.

Having children is a natural fulfillment of this need. As a team, parents give to each other so that they can more successfully give to the children.

Once children grow up and leave home, couples need to find a new goal or purpose. When we are serving the highest good of the family, community, or world as partners, our love can continue to grow without limit.

NOVEMBER 6

Why Men Are So Sensitive

You may be asking yourself why men are so sensitive about being asked for support. It is not because men are lazy but because men have so much need to feel accepted. Any request to be more or to give more might instead give the message that he is not accepted just the way he is.

If she wants more,
he gets the message that he is not enough.

Just as a woman is more sensitive about being heard and feeling understood when she is sharing her feelings, a man is more sensitive about being accepted just the way he is. Any attempt to improve him makes him feel as though you are trying to change him because he is not good enough.

On Mars, the motto is "Don't fix it unless it is broken." When a man feels that a woman wants more and that she is trying to change him, he receives the message that she feels he is broken. Naturally he doesn't feel loved just the way he is.

As women learn to ask for more in small increments and in a positive and nondemanding manner, men become much more receptive. Ultimately men are happiest when they feel they have succeeded in fulfilling the people they care about. By learning to ask for support correctly, a woman not only helps her man feel more loved but also ensures that she gets the loving support she wants, needs, and deserves.

NOVEMBER 7

Realizing the Potential of a Relationship

*T*oo many times we reject each other not because we have found that a person is wrong for us but because we believe something is wrong with that person. By ending relationships with a more loving and nonjudgmental attitude, we will continue to be attracted to the people who are closer to what we want. With this understanding, we find that we become less picky and more open to the potential of a relationship.

November 8

〜〜〜

The Male Need to Be Appreciated

The need for appreciation is generally confused with the need for respect. To appreciate a person is to acknowledge that what they do or how they express themselves is of value to you personally and that it is of some benefit. We need respect, on the other hand, to experience the validity of our needs, feelings, values, and rights. Appreciation is an act of evaluating, while respect validates.

> *Although women need appreciation, men particularly thrive on it and are most attracted to women who give it.*

Appreciation acknowledges that the value of our actions, intentions, results, and decisions—ultimately, our personal value, usefulness, and importance—has been seen. The feedback tells a man his behavior has served a purpose. If he can feel appreciated, then he is much more willing to explore and understand why some of his actions have failed.

Without appreciation, a person begins to feel inadequate and incapable of giving support. Without respect, a person may feel unworthy of receiving support.

Appreciation allows us to experience our intentions, decisions, and actions as valuable. It is the necessary support that inspires us to repeat an action that works or motivates us to change what doesn't work. Even when we fail to achieve our desired results, there is always something in what we did that can be appreciated.

NOVEMBER 9

Nongoal-Oriented Talking

*W*hen allowed to talk in a nonlinear, nongoal-oriented manner (pure Venusian), a woman can reconnect with her female side and can most effectively cope with the stress of working in a traditionally male role all day.

In conversation, if a man offers advice or tries to help a woman solve her problems, he is actually keeping her in her masculine side, which wants to solve problems. On the other hand, by allowing a woman to talk about problems without the urgency to solve them, he assists her in moving back toward speaking Venusian.

By simply responding with empathy, sympathy, and understanding, he nurtures her female side. With this kind of support, she is able to throw off her burdens and release her feelings of being overwhelmed. Gradually her energy returns, and her heart is full of appreciation and love.

If a woman is able to release her negative feelings in this way and not cling to them, it will assist a man in being more present in the relationship. It is sometimes particularly helpful for a man to initiate a conversation, because women today are so much in their male sides that they don't even know they need to talk until they are asked. If she has been burned in the past while sharing her feelings, she will not consciously feel the need to talk. With the clear signal of a man initiating the conversation, she does not have to fear his lack of interest in what she has to share.

NOVEMBER 10

Love Has No Requirements

*L*ove doesn't require you to be happy about everything your partner says and does. A woman can be loving and accepting and also express feelings of frustration, disappointment, concern, anger, hurt, sadness, and fear. She can be very happy some days and less happy on others. A part of her can be angry and yet another part happy to be with him. When she is in touch with her true feelings and needs, she is happy and appreciative, and those feelings will be real. Feelings, like the weather, are always changing. The contrasts allow us to appreciate the sunshine.

NOVEMBER 11

All Feelings Are Important

*I*f a woman is not supported in being unhappy, sometimes she can never truly be happy. To be genuinely happy requires dipping down into the well to release, heal, and purify the emotions. This is a natural and healthy process.

If we are to have the positive feelings of love, happiness, trust, and gratitude, we periodically also have to feel anger, sadness, fear, and sorrow. When a woman goes down into her well, she can heal these negative emotions. Men also need to process their negative feelings so that they can experience their positive feelings. A man goes into his cave to silently feel and process his negative feelings or release them with positive feelings.

Women are like waves. When a woman is on the upswing, she can be fulfilled with what she has, but on the downswing she then will become aware of what she is missing. When she is feeling good, she is capable of seeing and responding to the good things in her life. When she is crashing, her loving vision becomes cloudy, and she reacts more to what is missing in her life.

Just as a glass of water can be viewed as half full or half empty, when a woman is on her way up, she sees the fullness of her life. On the way down, she sees the emptiness. Whatever emptiness she overlooks on the way up comes into focus when she is on her way down into her well.

Without learning about how women are like waves, men can- not understand or support their wives. They are confused when things get a lot better on the outside but worse in the relation-ship. By remembering this difference, a man holds the key to giving his partner the love she deserves when she needs it the most.

NOVEMBER 12

❦

The Power of Forgiveness

*T*o open our hearts to each other and enjoy a lifetime of love, the most important skill of all is forgiveness. Forgiving your partner for their mistakes allows you to forgive yourself for not being perfect.

When we don't forgive in one relationship, our love is to various degrees restricted in our life relationships. We can still love others, but not as much. When a heart is blocked in one relationship, it beats more weakly in them all. Forgiving means letting go of hurt.

Forgiveness allows us to give our love again and helps us to open up to give and to receive love. When we are closed, we lose on two counts.

The more you love someone, the more you suffer when you don't forgive them. Many people are driven to suicide by the agonizing pain of not forgiving a loved one.

**The greatest pain we can ever feel is
the pain of not loving someone we love.**

We stubbornly hold on to bitterness and resentment, not because we are not loving but because we do not know how to forgive. If we were not loving, ceasing to love someone would not be painful at all. The more loving we are, the more painful it is not to forgive.

The power to forgive is within us all, but as is true with any other skill, we must practice it. In the beginning, it takes time. We work at forgiving our partner, and then we are blaming them again the next day. Mastering the new relationship skill of forgiveness takes time, but with practice it becomes a natural response.

The angels in heaven rejoice each time you forgive. When you choose to love instead of closing your heart, you bring a little spark of divinity into our dark world of struggle. You lighten the loads of others and help them to forgive as well.

NOVEMBER 13

The Male Need to Be Trusted

*T*rust is a firm belief in the ability, honesty, integrity, reliability, and sincerity of another person. The need to be trusted is the need for an acknowledgment from your partner that you are a good person—upstanding, you might say. When trust is absent, people consistently jump to the wrong, negative conclusion regarding a person's intent, whereas trust gives every offense the benefit of the doubt. Trust says, "There must be some good explanation for why this happened."

Trust grows in a relationship when each partner recognizes that the other does not intend to hurt, but seeks only to support.

A woman's trust in a man draws him to her. When a woman is trusting of a man, she is able to draw out the best in him. Of course, if she trusts him to be perfect, he will let her down. If she trusts that he can and will help, then he gets the message that he is of value and that his best is enough for her to accept and appreciate. Her trust will draw increasing greatness from him. With a woman's loving trust, a man is supported in realizing his powers, abilities, skills, and talents.

November 14

Complementary Needs

*S*oul mates basically have something that their partners need. When a man has what a woman needs, then she feels chemistry. For men, it is the other way around. When a woman needs what a man has to offer, he feels the chemistry. This mutual dependence creates healthy emotional chemistry.

Emotional chemistry frees us from being limited by our unrealistic pictures of what our ideal partner will look like or be like.

When a man is able to experience the thrill of feeling needed by a woman, he is no longer caught up in pictures and expectations of what his ideal partner should look like. He is released from judging her physical appearance when he enjoys the pleasure of making little romantic gestures and feeling her responses.

When a woman experiences a man treating her in a special way, she is free from fixating on how her ideal partner should look. By experiencing the chemistry that results from being receptive to a man's approach, she is free to follow her heart and not get caught up in unrealistic expectations of perfection.

NOVEMBER 15

Understanding Our Changes

*I*n many cases, when our partners change it is easy to misinterpret their motives and feel that they don't love us as much. Women commonly feel that they give but are not getting back. With greater insight, a woman's heart can be softened by the awareness that her man is trying to do his best but doesn't really grasp what she needs.

With a greater understanding of how a man's changes can affect the relationship, not only can a man make things better, but a woman is empowered to create the changes she wants. Besides learning how to interpret a man's changes correctly, women should also be aware of how they change in a relationship over the course of time. Just as men stop doing the little things, women will often take for granted the support they do provide.

NOVEMBER 16

Feeling Pain

*W*hen we are not getting the love we need but remain vulnerable to our partners, we feel pain. Many couples deal with this by numbing themselves. They might say to themselves "It doesn't matter, I don't care." They may begin to close up, saying "I can't really trust him to be there for me, so I won't rely on him."

The most painful and lonely feeling is lying next to someone you don't feel you can reach out and touch with love. At this point, you may turn to an addiction to avoid feeling the pain of not being loved. Such dependencies free us from the pain but kill the passion. Only by learning to reach out for love and ask for what we want in skillful ways can we really heal our pain.

By turning off our feelings, we lose touch with our inner passion. We may not even know what we actually need more of, because we have stopped feeling.

~~~

Finding Happiness in Reality

*I*t is not uncommon for a woman to feel she has a happy marriage and then, after ten years, wake up one day and realize how unhappy she has really been. She then rejects her partner for not fulfilling her. This blame is certainly her experience, but it is unfair. He is shocked when he finds that she is so unhappy. He says he is willing to change, and she says she is tired of trying to make the relationship work.

Her fatigue arises from years of trying to make it work by pretending that it was working. She was trying to be loving and nice when deep inside a resentment was growing.

> **For years a woman may appear happy and fulfilled and then suddenly be resentful or depressed.**

Some women spend years living in the future, denying the pain in the present, while others go through much shorter cycles. A woman may flip from elation to depression in one week, twice a month, or once in ten or twenty years. The longer she denies her pain, the greater her depression when it comes up.

In most cases, when a woman discovers that she is not getting what she needs, she feels like a victim. She blames her husband rather than taking responsibility for the mixed messages she was sending the whole time. When she does wake up, in order to find balance she has a valid need to feel like a victim for a while. Then she can work on taking responsibility.

NOVEMBER 18

When She Is Receptive, He Will Thrive

*W*hen a woman is receptively interested in a man, he thrives. When she reacts to his advances, he feels more connected to her. When a man feels more connected, he is automatically more interested and motivated to get to know her. A woman's receptive interest is fertile ground where the seed of a man's interest can grow.

NOVEMBER 19

The Symptoms of Stress

*T*here are three major symptoms of stress in men. It is important to recognize these symptoms because women tend to take them personally and mistakenly assume matters are worse than they are. These three symptoms of stress are withdrawing, grumbling, and shutting down. When this happens, a woman generally feels unloved and afraid that the relationship is in trouble. A correct interpretation of these symptoms can help a woman relax and more skillfully support her partner in coping with stress and coming back into balance.

Likewise, there are three major indications of stress in women that men tend to take personally and misinterpret. Her symptoms of stress are feeling overwhelmed, overreacting, and exhaustion. When a woman gets upset, instead of knowing how to support her, a man usually gets upset that *she* is upset, making matters worse. By learning to recognize these stress reactions and interpret them correctly, men can also relax more and learn how to better support their partners.

NOVEMBER 20

How We Find Our Partners

*F*inding a partner is like any other skill in life; it takes talent, education, and practice. The more information, education, and experience you have, the better off you will be. By gaining all three, you stand the greatest chance of mastering a skill.

It is the same in marriage. Some couples just start out great; others take time to overcome and harmonize their differences; and others experience a beakthrough after a long stuggle and experience the joys of lasting romance.

Self-Blame vs. Blaming Others

*W*omen tend to blame themselves first, while men first blame others. Whenever there is a problem, conflict, or negative experience, women tend to feel too much responsibility. They see themselves as responsible first, and then they recognize how others share in the responsibility. They are especially hard on and judgmental of themselves before they look to see how others contributed to the problem.

Men, on the other hand, are likely to accuse others before they look at their responsibility for problems. They tend to be immediately aware of the shortcomings of others before becoming aware of their own.

A man sees problems as obstacles to achieving a particular outcome or goal. From this focused perspective, any obstruction is perceived first with blame.

> **It is not that men are less responsible; they just look first outside themselves for the problem and then to themselves.**

A woman sees problems in a larger context—as outcomes that need to be corrected. From this perspective, a woman is quick to see all the possible ways she could have done something differently in order to have produced a different outcome. Thus she easily feels responsible and accepts blame.

These basic differences give rise to much confusion in relationships. When a man reacts to a problem with blame, the woman mistakenly assumes that he has already considered his responsibility first as a woman would do, and that his final conclusion is that she is at fault. This gives the impact of his blame much more weight than it really carries. If she can learn not to react defensively to his blame, she gives him a chance to cool down and explore his own responsibility.

NOVEMBER 22

Lightness and Fun

A man is almost always annoyed when a woman wants to "work on the relationship." He doesn't want to work on it. He would rather just live in it.

A man needs to feel that sometimes he is on vacation in the relationship and, in a sense, can do no wrong. He wants to feel that he is fine the way he is and that he is not required to change. When a woman says, "It's no big deal" or "It's okay," he tends to light up.

When a woman can be lighthearted about her problems,
a man feels like a success.

On the other hand, for a woman to feel friendship for a man means that he can be relaxed about her getting upset. If he can just give her a little sympathy without taking the issue so personally, she can shift her feelings without making a scene.

Friendship for a woman means that her mate will go out of his way to support her or offer his help from time to time. Friendship for a man means that a woman will go out of her way not to be demanding or expect too much.

Being our partner's friend means never trying to change their mood or taking it personally when our mate is not feeling the way we would like. Learning this lesson of detachment can totally transform the relationship.

NOVEMBER 23

A Woman's Responsibility

*I*t is a woman's responsibility to find, again and again, that trusting part of her. Men have to share in this responsibility by earning a woman's trust. If a man hurts a woman without apologizing, he is unknowingly building walls. Most of the time a man doesn't realize the importance of compassion or an apology. When a man doesn't give an apology, the wise woman will let a man know what she needs to hear.

NOVEMBER 24

Staying Open

*T*he challenge women face in their relationships is to keep opening up when feeling disappointed or unloved. It is of paramount importance that they work on trusting their partners more and more and continue to be receptive. Otherwise they will lose touch with their vulnerability and needs.

The secret to growing in trust is not to expect your partner to be perfect but to believe that he cares. By understanding how men are different, a woman can trust that he loves her even when he doesn't do the things she would do to demonstrate caring.

Over time, she can begin to see the ways in which he thinks he is loving her. Most important, she can apply advanced relationship skills to help him be more successful in supporting her.

Women need to work on trusting,
while men need to work on caring.

To take down the wall around his heart, a man must work on caring. To bring back the passion, he needs to remember that it will require hard work and effort. At times it will be like lifting a heavy weight.

If there is no wall around his heart, doing things is easy. Once he is taken for granted, the wall begins to rise again. Each time he feels his efforts are not appreciated, another brick is added to the wall.

As he consciously begins doing little things that she can appreciate, if only for brief moments, the wall-building stops. When his determination frays, and the wall suddenly looks higher, he becomes wary and resistant once more. He craves only to spend a lot of time in his cave.

A man can eventually come out and overcome the inertia of not caring if he is aware of the efforts required to open his heart again. As he does, he will see that he is becoming a stronger person. With this strength, his road ahead will be less rocky. Eventually he will be energized as never before by pleasing his partner.

NOVEMBER 25

How Men and Women React Differently to Stress

*M*asculine awareness is primarily concerned with what happens in the outer world: by changing the outside objective world, the masculine nature attempts to reduce stress. A man reacts to stress by withdrawing into his thoughts to determine what needs to be done to reduce the stress.

When a man reacts to stress from his feminine, emotional side, he tends to lose his positive attitudes. His negative emotions may make him destructive, moody, and self-centered. Negative emotions are not bad. They are a part of healing or de-stressing. When a man experiences his negative emotions and has lost his objectivity, his emotions become mean, threatening, and unloving.

The feminine psyche is more concerned with the inner subjective world: the feminine psyche attempts to reduce stress by changing herself. A woman primarily reacts to stress with an upsurge of feelings. These feelings allow her to center herself, explore her attitudes, and make changes within herself so that she can reduce her stress. For example, if something is upsetting her, she can reduce her stress by becoming more flexible, tolerant, forgiving, patient, understanding. By changing her attitude, she reduces stress and feels better.

As long as a woman is in touch with her positive feelings and attitudes, her thinking will be clear and flexible. As long as a man's thinking and attitudes are positive, his feelings will be loving and supportive.

꧁꧂

It Is Normal to Make Mistakes

*I*t is normal to make mistakes in finding the right person for you. Once you are in a relationship, it is still normal to make mistakes. The difference between success and failure is being able to learn from our mistakes to become more discerning. If you want to hit a home run, the chances of striking out go up dramatically. Babe Ruth, who held the record for the most home runs, also held the record for the most strikeouts.

If you want your relationship to be more than what previous generations have experienced, then new skills must be learned. If you want to run fast, then your chances of falling also increase. The secret of success is to get up and keep going. You can do it. Once it happens, you will look back and realize that it happened at the right time for you.

Dealing with Anger

*W*hen a man is angry it is easy for him to lose control and become violent, break things, or say cruel things. This is his dark side. It is esssential that men learn the importance of containment. It is not appropriate for men to be encouraged to express their feelings freely without first considering them.

If a man is to express angry feelings, it is best he share them with someone with whom he is not angry. If he is angry and someone is resistant to hearing what he has to say, he will say and do things that he will regret later. Put very simply, men have less impulse control than women and tend to act out their feelings. Women tend to talk out their feelings and maintain greater control. This is not an excuse for losing control. A man is responsible for his actions regardless of how angry he becomes.

> **When a man becomes angry,**
> **it is his responsibility to take a time-out to cool off.**

As a basic guideline, a man needs to remember that if he speaks or makes a decision when he is angry, he will always lose. With this insight, women can be careful to give a man a lot of space when he is angry. It is not the time to draw him out, make decisions, or get him to talk. Once he has cooled off is the time to have a conversation.

Freedom to Say No

A relationship is healthy when both partners have permission to ask for what they want and need, and to say no if they choose. We can feel free to ask for what we want only if we know that our partner feels comfortable saying no. This way both partners learn to depend on each other, yet trust that when their partner says no, they are still doing their best.

November 29

Healthy Dependence

*A*s we grow together in love and trust, we open up and feel our mutual needs more strongly. Passion is most powerfully experienced when we need someone and can trust that person to be there for us. At the same time, passion is extinguished when we become too dependent.

It is unwise as well as naive to expect our partners always to give us the love we need. Sometimes they have none to share, yet we demand more. This is like saying to a person in a wheelchair, "If you love me, then you will stand up and walk."

Sometimes our partners just can't be there for us in the ways we think they can and should. Once we begin to need our partners in ways in which they can't or don't support us, we will not only turn them off but disappoint ourselves as well. When we need our partners too much, we will eventually withdraw our trust and caring. We set them up to fail.

By adjusting our expectations, we can be much more successful in fulfilling and trusting each other. With this kind of trust, even when our partners let us down, we will know that they did the best they could. This wise attitude allows us to be much more forgiving.

NOVEMBER 30

Good Endings Make Good Beginnings

*H*ow we end a relationship and how we evaluate a date are essential to fine-tuning our ability to be attracted to the right person for us. The secret of making sure one relationship leads you to another one closer to what you want is to pay a lot of attention to how you end a relationship.

How you end a relationship has an enormous impact on the quality of your next relationship.

Good endings make good beginnings. When you end a relationship feeling either resentful or guilty, it is much harder to move on to find a person who is right for you. But when a relationship ends, we often may feel angry that our partner let us down or didn't fulfill our expectations.

Women most commonly feel that they gave a lot to a relationship and didn't get what they needed in return. As a result they feel resentful. Men, on the other hand, tend to feel more guilty. They feel bad that the relationship didn't turn out well and guilty if their partner felt unfulfilled.

Although these dynamics are common, it can also be the other way around. Generally the person who feels most rejected or abandoned feels resentful. The rejecter feels guilty. In either case, the result is the same. We end a relationship with a closed heart.

Without an open heart, it is much more difficult to find love again.

When our hearts are open, we are able to be attracted to and even to fall in love with the right person, or at least make progress in finding someone closer to the right person. When our hearts are open, we can be assured that we are getting closer to our goal. When our hearts are closed, we tend to repeat the same experiences.

In a marriage, the same principles apply. When we are unable to resolve painful issues and release resentments and guilt, we block the growth of love. When love is blocked, we begin to doubt our partner. To bring out the best in our partner and see them as the right choice, we must take responsibility to remove the blocks we have created. By letting go of resentment and guilt, we are free once more to feel and experience true and lasting love.

❧ DECEMBER ❧

Give, Nurture, Love

*A*nother full year will soon close. My hope for you is that it has been a year in which you have felt your love more deeply. The path toward growth and understanding is the road of life itself.

Love is the central need, and the road to greater love begins with loving yourself. Before we can freely and fully give unconditional love, we must learn to receive from others as well as ourselves.

Even when we are loving ourselves, relationships are not easy. Humans have myriad needs to be filled. Bringing our lives together and keeping romance requires not only the best we have within us but also new insights and skills.

Never forget that your ability to love is the most precious gift you have. Don't waste it. Use every moment of your life as an opportunity to give and receive love. Soon you'll notice that life has ceased to be a struggle. When your heart is filled with love, life becomes a vacation.

Dedicate yourself to making love work in your life and in the world, and the rewards for yourself and those you love will be priceless. By keeping your promise to love and nurture your partner above all else, you are able to open your heart again and again.

In spiritual terms, the desire to be married is our soul remembering the sacred promise we are here to keep. It is God's will within us being felt. When we fully commit ourselves to keeping that promise, we align ourselves with God's will.

All the pieces in our lives begin to fit together when our hearts are open. By making sure we keep our soul's promise, we are able to bring the spiritual into the material world. When we live in love, we bring the kingdom of heaven on earth.

DECEMBER 1

ᡊᡊᡊ

Love: The Central Need

*A*s human beings, we are incredibly complex, with an endless stream of physical, emotional, mental, and spiritual needs that must be satisfied. Frustration at any of these levels can produce suffering for the whole being. There is one need so fundamental and essential that when it is not met, it causes everything else to fail or fall short of fulfillment. That is the need for love—love of others and love of yourself.

Without love, we end up creating all sorts of other problems.

The major cause of human dissatisfaction and frustration is the absence of love. This fundamental human need outweighs all others. Without love, you can never feel a genuine sense of fulfillment. It is the foundation of security upon which you can build a successful life. No matter what you possess, you cannot fully enjoy it unless you are loving yourself and sharing with people you care about. No matter how much you accomplish or acquire in life, it cannot supersede your basic need for love.

DECEMBER 2

The Union of Soul Mates

*O*ur soul mate embodies qualities and attributes we unconsciously seek to find within ourselves. By loving this person, we begin to accept and awaken those same qualities hidden within our own being. This discovery of self brings us greater fulfillment.

We seek union with our soul mate to experience a greater wholeness within ourselves. As we grow in wholeness, we feel more certain that our relationship was meant to be. Although our partner is not perfect, we have found that special person with whom we are to share our lives, as if ordained by the heavens.

DECEMBER 3

Emotional Housekeeping

*W*hen a woman's wave crashes, it is a time of emotional cleansing or emotional housecleaning. Without this cleansing or emotional catharsis, a woman slowly loses her ability to love and to grow in love. Through controlled repression of her feelings, her wave nature is obstructed, and over time she gradually becomes unfeeling and passionless.

Even a strong, confident, and successful woman will need to visit her well from time to time. Men commonly make the mistake of thinking that if their female partner is successful in the work world, then she will not experience these times of emotional housecleaning. The opposite is true.

When a woman is in the work world, she generally is exposed to stress and emotional pollution. Her need for emotional house-cleaning is just postponed. When a woman puts on her business suit, she can detach from this emotional roller coaster, but when she returns home she needs her partner to give the tender loving support that every woman needs and appreciates.

It is important to recognize that this tendency to go into the well does not necessarily affect a woman's competence at work, but it does greatly influence her communication with the people she intimately loves and needs.

DECEMBER 4

Great Sex for the Relationship

Great sex reminds men and women of the tender and highest love that originally drew them together. The alchemy of great sex generates the chemicals in the brain and body that allow the fullest enjoyment of one's partner. Sex increases our attraction to each other, stimulates greater energy, and even promotes better health. It leaves us not only with the sparkle of youthful vitality but also with a heightened sense of beauty, wonder, and appreciation for each other and the world around us. Great sex is God's special gift to those who work hard to make love a priority in their lives.

DECEMBER 5

Getting to the Goal vs. Enjoying the Ride

When a woman is overwhelmed from her day, it is more difficult for her to relax enough to have a sexual climax. At these times, what she needs is to be cuddled. She needs lots of hugs, affection, and intimate embracing. When she is held and loved in a nonsexual way, she can relax without any demands being made of her. This is a heavenly experience for her and is closely related to how men feel after they have a climax.

It is important to understand this feminine need; otherwise men don't take the time to give this kind of loving support to their partners. This nonsexual, nongoal-oriented physical touching is highly valued by women in ways that men do not understand. Touching is as important to women as sex is to men.

DECEMBER 6

⁂

Successful Giving and Receiving

*B*y improving communication, a man can learn to be more effective in supporting his partner, without being overworked himself. At each step, her appreciation will motivate him to do more. It will not entail a major sacrifice, nor will he feel controlled.

Men want to be the providers; they want to take credit for a woman's happiness; and they thrive on feeling successful in making a difference. They just need to feel appreciated for it. This is the kind of love and support that a man craves most from a woman.

Men and women complement each other in a very magical way. Men thrive on successfully caring for their partners, while women thrive when they feel cared for. Certainly women also love to care for their male partners, but they primarily need to feel cared for themselves. I have never heard a woman say, "My partner completely ignores me, but I still love giving to him."

DECEMBER 7

How a Man Feels Love

A man is free to feel when he has achieved his goal. When his male side has done its work successfully, he swings over to his female side and feels fully. When he can satisfy his own desires and also fulfill his partner, he can relax and feel a greater sense of peace, love, and joy.

In a way, when he and his partner experience an orgasm, he feels he has completed his job and has been richly rewarded by her deeply felt appreciation and love for him.

By giving her an orgasm first, a man opens a woman up to respond fully to his orgasm. After she has experienced her orgasm, she can best share the fullness of her love and receptivity. At the moment of his climax, he is able to fully join with her and receive the love she has for him. To whatever extent his partner loves him, at this precious moment he is able to let it in the most.

When he knows she is fulfilled and appreciative of him, he can thrive in that moment. More than at any other time, he can let her love in, feel the love deep in his heart, and reaffirm his commitment to her.

꩜

Love Motivates Martians

*W*hen a man is in love, he is motivated to be the best he can be in order to serve others. When his heart is open, he feels so confident in himself that he is capable of making major changes. Given the opportunity to prove his potential, he expresses his best self. Only when he feels he cannot succeed does he regress back to his old selfish ways.

When a man is in love, he begins to care about another as much as himself. He is suddenly released from the binding chains of being motivated by himself alone and becomes free to give to another, not for personal gain but out of caring. He experiences his partner's fulfillment as if it were his own. He can easily endure any hardship to make her happy because her happiness makes him happy. His struggles become easier. He is energized with a higher purpose.

In his youth, he can be satisfied by serving himself alone. As he matures, self-gratification is no longer as satisfying. To experience fulfillment, he must begin to live his life motivated by love. Being inspired to give in such a free and selfless way liberates him from the inertia of self-gratification devoid of caring for others. Although he still needs to receive love, his greatest need is to give love.

DECEMBER 9

～✥～

The Need to Be Cared For

*R*elationships are an ongoing process of giving, receiving, and sharing. The success of a relationship is based on our ability to give of ourselves. Our ability to give is directly related to our ability to receive. One cannot continue to give unless one is also receiving support.

It is essential that those with whom we are in relationships be responsive to and care about our needs to the best of their ability. A caring attitude allows us to open up and trust that we are special and entitled to receive support.

DECEMBER 10

～✥～

How Men Receive Love Differently

*T*hrough his actions, a man can most directly connect to his feelings. When his actions are acknowledged and appreciated, he feels most loved. This acceptance frees him to experience the fullness of feeling loved and in return to become more loving. Women do not instinctively understand this, because their feelings are directly connected to the brain's talking centers.

A woman feels loved by the way she is treated. When she feels heard and understood, she feels loved. When her needs are recognized and supported, she feels loved.

Women mistakenly give the kind of loving support they want themselves. When a man is distressed, women think they are being loving by trying to get him to talk. A woman does not realize that the best thing she can do is to accept him by giving him lots of space. When he is out of his cave, she can respond warmly in a way that says she is glad to have him in her life. With this new awareness of how men feel loved, women can begin to focus their support in ways that matter most to their mates.

DECEMBER 11

Practice Makes Perfect

*J*ust as a man needs to listen and respond to her needs and requests in whatever way he can, the best way a woman can create romance is not to take anything he does for her for granted. Certainly there will be times when she doesn't respond with appreciation, just as there will be times when he doesn't respond immediately to her requests, but by being aware of these basic dynamics at work, they will always be moving in the right direction.

As couples practice keeping romance alive, it actually gets easier and easier. When a man anticipates that he will be appreciated for doing something, he has more energy to do it. When a woman anticipates that he will hear her and respond with consideration, she feels much more appreciative and can more easily acknowledge all he does. And she can be more forgiving at those times when he makes mistakes or seems self-centered or lazy.

> *When a man anticipates that he will be appreciated for doing something, he has more energy to do it.*

When a woman consistently lets a man know what a great guy he is for the little things he does, he will continue to do them. It brings out the best in him. Without her support, he may regress back to focusing only on the big things like making money and being a good provider. When he does little things for her, it gives her the chance to feel her love for him again and again.

Romantic rituals take time to develop, but each time a man gets into the habit of doing something a woman likes, and she continues to express her appreciation instead of taking it for granted, he will automatically be motivated to do a little more.

DECEMBER 12

Practicing Compassion

*A*s we struggle to understand the different ways our partners think and feel, we can begin to realize how difficult it must be for them to understand us. As we experience frustration and disappointment, we can use our experience to imagine how our partner must feel as well. Learning to create intimacy is challenging for both sexes. With this insight, we can practice being compassionate.

Men, if you experience frustration trying to listen to your partner, recognize that the frustration you are feeling is what she is feeling. Although you may not understand fully why she feels this way, at least recognize with compassion that this is what she is feeling too.

No one is perfect. Even though these Mars/Venus principles of making relationships work are simple, they are also difficult to remember and put into practice. Lasting change takes time. When your partner disappoints you, rather than getting caught up in feeling upset, give youself a break by giving your partner a break. Practice compassion for your partner and yourself. Compassion creates an understanding warmth that allows us to accept our partner's limitations and mistakes.

DECEMBER 13

※

Why Women Feel They Give More

*W*omen today feel they give more, and they expect men to give back more in return. While this is true, there is another perspective. Though he may be giving less than she is, he is not giving less than men in the past have given. He is giving what men have always given. By understanding this problem from both perspectives and without blame, men and women can be motivated to solve their share of the problem.

To solve this basic problem, we must first recognize that it is not really about how much more she does. Instead it is about what she is not getting in order to be fulfilled. Regardless of how much a woman does, she will find greater balance, energy, and love in a relationship with better communication. Rather than focusing on what a man is doing or not doing, it is wiser to focus on a woman's need to be heard.

> *When a woman experiences good communication*
> *and great sex, it is not so important*
> *how much a man helps out in the home.*

As men learn how to provide emotional support by using new relationship skills, then and only then will women begin to feel greater warmth and appreciation. This warmth and appreciation open the door for more romance and sex. With good communication and regular great sex, it doesn't matter so much how much a man helps out around the house.

Ironically, at that point when a woman truly feels more centered and appreciative, a man is naturally motivated gradually to do more in the home. A man can and will give more at home, but this change takes time. Just as a weight-lifter gradually builds muscle by slowly increasing his weights, a man can change gradually. The first step is improving communication, then creating regular great sex, and then, as a result, a man finds the energy and motivation to help out more in the home.

DECEMBER 14

The Twelve Kinds of Love

*M*ost of our complex emotional needs can be summarized as the need for love. Men and women each have six unique love needs that are all equally important. Men primarily need trust, acceptance, appreciation, admiration, approval, and encouragement. Women primarily need caring, understanding, respect, devotion, validation, and reassurance. The enormous task of figuring out what our partner needs is simplified greatly by understanding these twelve kinds of love.

It is easy for a woman to give what she needs and forget that her favorite Martian may need something else. Likewise, men tend to focus on their needs, losing track of the fact that the kind of love they need is not always appropriate for or supportive of their favorite Venusian.

The most powerful and practical aspect of this new understanding is that these different kinds of love are reciprocal. For example, when a Martian expresses his caring and understanding, a Venusian automatically begins to reciprocate and return to him the trust and acceptance he primarily needs. The same thing happens when a Venusian expresses her trust—a Martian automatically begins to reciprocate with the caring she needs.

DECEMBER 15

The Logistics of Foreplay

*B*ecause their awareness is so expanded and open, women are easily distracted or affected by their environment, especially when it comes to their own needs. When it is her time to relax and enjoy, a woman may find herself worrying about unpaid bills or wondering if the house is safe.

Men need to recognize that the environment is essential to the lovemaking process for women. Beautiful surroundings go a long way. Lighting a candle, sweet smells, low light, soft music—all make a tremendous difference.

DECEMBER 16

~⚜~

Symbols of Love

A woman needs symbols of love. When a man brings a woman flowers, for example, they validate the value of her beauty and femininity. Women need to be given flowers on an ongoing basis. To a woman, flowers are symbols of a man's love. They make his love concrete. It is unfortunate when a man assumes that she will tire of them and stops giving them to her.

Big presents or very little presents, all serve a very important romantic function. They help a woman know that she is special. She feels special when he treats her in a special way. Giving presents is a way of honoring a woman's need to be reassured.

Little notes are also effective symbols of love. They are affectionate reminders that simply reassure. It is not necessary to be original or even creative. Just say the basics, over and over again. As long as your notes express what you feel, they will be effective. Some of the basic reminders are: I love you; I miss you; You are the delight of my life; Just a reminder to say I care.

꧁꧂

Pleasing Her

A woman needs to remember that she is the jewel and that a man provides the right setting for her to shine. Instead of focusing on pleasing him because he makes her so happy, she needs to let him continue to please her with his actions. Instead of always stopping her life for him, she needs to let him demonstrate his interest by making adjustments in his schedule for her.

When a woman allows a man to make little sacrifices for her, not only does she feel more special, but he also feels that she is more special. When a man puts his love into action, he always feels his love more strongly. By letting a man do things for her, a woman becomes more attractive to a man.

When a man is in pursuit, a woman does not have to do anything to earn his interest. He is already interested. The more he gives and she graciously receives, the more interested he becomes. Without this insight, a woman can unknowingly prevent a man from wanting more of her by giving too much in reaction, being too eager to please, too enthusiastic, too accommodating, and too available. When a man feels he is winning a woman, she becomes increasingly attractive.

DECEMBER 18

꧁꧂

When a Woman Is on Her Male Side

*W*hen a woman is too much on her male side, the antidote is to create relationships in which her female side blossoms. Yet if she works in a traditionally male role all day, she will have to make deliberate efforts to overcome an inner resistance. Though it is easy for many women to become more masculine, it is generally difficult to come back to their female side.

When a woman on her masculine side gets home, she may want to go to her cave. She is definitely not in a communicative mood. She feels a much greater need for space than her man does. She needs to solve problems and can't waste time talking about them. In most cases, she would rather do things herself. She definitely feels that her partner isn't giving her the appreciation she deserves as a co-provider.

Since her male side wants to be appreciated, accepted, and trusted, she may resent her partner's need to be appreciated and demand that she wants it, too. Competing with her partner for appreciation is a no-win situation. It is like a man competing with a woman to be heard. Every woman knows what a turnoff it is when a man dominates a conversation and wants to be heard. Likewise, a man is turned off when a woman demands to be appreciated.

Competing with her partner for appreciation is a no-win situation.

Often when a woman is feeling the need for appreciation, it is a sign that she is on her male side. Deep inside, what she needs first is help in most cases. She needs a cooperative, caring, and supportive partner. The most immediate way to feel that support and come back to her female side is to improve communication.

By focusing on communication, she can shift from needing to solve the problems at home to sharing feelings about the problems. When she opens up to sharing, her female side is nurtured and she will be centered and fulfilled. Instead of needing to be appreciated, she will appreciate her partner for being there for her.

To avoid competing with her partner for appreciation, ideally a woman should look to the man in her life primarily for caring, understanding, and respect. These qualities of love nurture her female side. As she gets those needs fulfilled and her appreciation for her partner increases, she can expect that he will overflow and appreciate all that she does as well. Meanwhile, to support her male side, she needs to spend time with other women who can fulfill her need to be appreciated.

How You May Be Unknowingly Turning Off Your Partner

*W*ithout an awareness of what is important for the opposite sex, we don't realize how much we may be hurting our partners. Men and women get their feelings hurt most easily when they don't get the kind of love they need on their planet. Women generally don't realize the ways they communicate that are unsupportive and hurtful to men. Even though a woman may try to be considerate, she may unknowingly turn a man off.

> **By understanding a man's primary love needs, a woman can be more aware of the sources of his discontent.**

Just as women easily make mistakes when they don't understand what men primarily need, men also make mistakes. Men generally don't recognize the ways they communicate that are disrespectful and unsupportive of women. A man may even know that she is unhappy with him, but unless he understands why she feels unloved and what she needs, he cannot change his approach. By understanding a woman's primary needs, a man can be more sensitive to and respectful of her needs.

꩜

Giving Support at Difficult Times

*E*very relationship has difficult times. They may occur for a variety of reasons—the loss of a job, a death or illness in the family, over-spending and debt, increasing stress, too much to do, or just not enough rest. At these difficult times, the important thing is to try to communicate with a loving, validating, and approving attitude.

We need to accept and understand that we and our partners will not always be perfect. By learning to communicate successfully in response to the smaller upsets in a relationship, you will find it easier to deal with the bigger challenges when they suddenly appear.

Take some time when you are not upset with your partner to discover what words work best to signal the need for a time-out. Find out what works for your partner, and share what works best for you. Adopting a few prearranged statements can be immensely helpful to neutralize tension when a time-out is needed.

Sometimes the best solution for avoiding conflict is to see it coming and lie low for a while. Take a time-out to center yourself so that you can then come together again with greater understanding, acceptance, validation, and approval.

✷

Every Relationship Is a Gift

*E*very relationship is a gift, offering us the opportunity to prepare ourselves to find and recognize our soul mate. Each time you do your best to love a partner and then take time to end a relationship with forgiveness, you are increasing your ability to discern the right person for you. Good endings make for good beginnings.

Each time, you gain the ability to shoot your arrow closer to the target. When a relationship ends, it is good to take some time to reflect on the gift and then begin again. When you feel grateful for something, then you are ready to move on.

Even divorce can give us the gift of discernment. If we take the time to forgive our partner and ourselves for our mistakes, then our next relationship can bring us closer to the mark. By finding the gift or the good in each relationship, we will eventually make our dreams come true.

This same principle applies to all our relationships. By taking the time to forgive and let go, we are ensuring that we continue to grow in love in all our relationships.

The Winter of Love

*D*uring the cold, barren months of winter, all of nature pulls back within itself. It is a time of rest, reflection, and renewal. This is a time in relationships when we experience our own unresolved pain or our shadow self. It is when our lid comes off and our painful feelings emerge. It is a time of solitary growth when we need to look more to ourselves than to our partners for love and fulfillment. It is a time of healing. This is the time when men hibernate in their caves and women sink to the bottom of their wells.

To sustain growth in love even through the winter of love, we need to be prepared by having lots of friends and family to support us. When it seems as if our partner cannot or is not supporting us, that is the time to support ourselves and get support from others. As we fill up inside without being dependent on our partners, another shift takes place. The winter of love passes, and spring returns.

After we have loved and healed ourselves through the dark winter of love, spring inevitably returns. Once again we are blessed with the feelings of hope, love, and an abundance of possibilities. Based on the inner healing and soul-searching of our wintry journey, we are able to open our hearts and feel the springtime of love.

DECEMBER 23

God Helps Those Who Help Themselves

*P*eople attribute finding their soul mates solely to chance, fate, luck, magic, good fortune, or God's grace because they don't realize how it actually happens. Certainly everything great happens with God's help, but God helps those who help themselves. Every day, without knowing what they are doing, individuals happen to do the right things to find a soul mate. They put themselves in the right place at the right time, and then it can happen miraculously.

Even when the fruit is ripe, we still need to find it and pick it. In a similar way, to find our soul mates we need to be ready, but we also need to be in the right place. Whether intentionally or unintentionally, these people put themselves in environments that allowed them to meet a potential partner with whom they felt immediate chemistry. To increase your chances of finding love, change your habits and routines. Even visit places where you would not expect to find love.

When we are married, the same principle applies. We may love our partners, but we don't create opportunities for that love to be felt. Routine kills passion. Take time to do new things. Change your habits and routines. Go different places and do different things together and also alone.

December 24

The Gift of Love

Solving the mystery of love can be the most exciting adventure of your life. It takes a willingness always to stay in touch with your feelings and to tell the complete truth about them to yourself and others. Let your commitment to the truth be a turning point in your life.

The more you tell the truth in your life, the more you will learn to trust your feelings and enjoy them. With practice, you can learn to ride the waves of feelings without getting stuck or needing to suppress any of your emotions.

Your ability to love is the most precious gift you have. Don't waste it. Use every moment of your life as an opportunity to give and receive love. Soon you'll notice that life has ceased to be a struggle.

Love can work if you know how to make it work, and now you do. Dedicate yourself to making love work in your life and in the world, and the rewards for yourself and those you love will be priceless.

꧁꧂

How We Express Our Soul

*T*he desire to share our life with someone is the expression of our soul. In practical terms, it is our soul remembering its highest purpose. By making a commitment to fulfill that purpose, we align ourselves with the power within us to be successful, not only in our marriage but in our life as well.

In spiritual terms, the desire to be married is our soul remembering the sacred promise we are here to keep. It is God's will within us being felt. When we fully commit ourselves to keeping that promise, we align ourselves with God's will.

All the pieces in our lives begin to fit together when our hearts are open. By keeping our promise to love and cherish our partner above all else, we are able to open our hearts again and again. By making sure we keep our soul's promise, we are able to bring the spiritual into the material world. When we live in love, we bring the kingdom of heaven on earth.

How to Ask for Support and Get It

*I*f you are not getting the support you want in your relationships, a significant reason may be that you do not ask enough or that you ask in a way that doesn't work. Asking for love and support is essential to the success of any relationship. If you want to G-E-T, then you have to A-S-K.

There are five secrets to asking a Martian for support successfully:

1. *Appropriate timing*—Beware of asking him to do something that he is obviously just planning to do. For example, if he is about to empty the trash, don't say, "Could you empty the trash?" He will feel you are telling him what to do. Timing is crucial. Also, if he is fully focused on something, don't expect him to respond to your request immediately.

2. *Nondemanding attitude*—Remember that a request is not a demand. If you have a resentful or demanding attitude, no matter how carefully you choose your words he will feel unappreciated for what he has already given and will probably say no.

3. *Brevity*—Avoid giving him a list of reasons why he should help you. Assume that he doesn't have to be convinced. The longer

you explain yourself, the more he will resist. Long explanations make him feel as though you don't trust him to support you. He will start to feel manipulated instead of free to offer his support.

4. *Directness*—Women often think they are asking for support when they are not. When a woman needs support, she may present the problem but not ask for a man's support. She expects him to offer his support and neglects to ask for it directly. In other words, she implies the request but does not directly state it. These indirect requests make a man feel taken for granted and unappreciated.

5. *Correct wording*—One of the most common mistakes in asking for support is use of the words "could" and "can" in place of "would" and "will." "Could you empty the trash?" is merely a question gathering information. "Would you empty the trash?" is a request. On Mars it would be an insult to ask a man "Can you empty the trash?" Of course he can empty the trash! The question is not *can* he empty the trash, but *will* he empty the trash. Because he feels insulted, he may say no just because you have irritated him.

When you ask a man for support and you do not reject him for saying no, he will remember that, and next time he will be much more willing to give. On the other hand, if you quietly sacrifice your needs and don't ask, he won't have any idea how many times he is needed. How can he know if you don't ask?

~~~

Love and Need

*W*hen we give to ourselves, we experience fulfillment, but when we give to someone we love, our fulfillment is expanded. When our hearts are open, what we give always comes back to us. Our partner's joy becomes our joy. By giving with an open heart, we experience a much greater joy in our lives.

When love is not joyful, we are confused about it. When love is difficult or a strain, we are demanding too much from our partners. It is easy to confuse love with need. We get things backward. We assume that needing more from our partners is an expression of our love. It is not.

> **Real love does not make demands;**
> **it is open and generous, free and accepting.**

When we are needing and demanding more from our partners, we must recognize that although it may feel as if we are being loving, we are not. Love does not make demands. Love extends itself, embraces, and forgives. Although we may love our partner, when we are needing more than they can offer, we have lost touch with genuine loving feelings and are caught up in our needs.

By recognizing that we are not loving, we can focus on finding our love again. When we approach our partner with the openness of love, we will always be more successful in asking for and getting more of what we need and want in a relationship. Finding our love again is easier when we are able to identify when we have stopped loving. Being responsible to come back to loving feelings automatically motivates our partner to give more.

DECEMBER 28

The Seed of Greatness

*T*he seed of greatness is our ability to know, speak, and keep our word or our truth. One power is to keep our word by doing what we say we will do. Another power is to support the people we care about most. Another power is to uphold and live in accordance with what we believe to be right and just. The highest power is to act, feel, and think from an open heart. When our hearts are open, we are able to act in accordance with our highest purpose, which is to love.

When we can do what we say we are going to do, we gradually find the power to manifest our dreams. When we can express the best of who we are, we gradually create the good fortune to attract in our lives all the opportunities we need. When we can act, feel, and think in accordance with what our soul wants to do, we can manifest greatness in our everyday lives.

By keeping our soul's promise, we infuse our lives with meaning, grace, and purpose. Marriage is the acknowledgment of that promise, and making sure a marriage works is the fulfillment of one of our soul's highest purposes. By making this commitment, we harness our inner power to make love last in our lives.

DECEMBER 29

When a Man Takes Charge

A woman loves it when a man takes charge and follows through to do something without dropping it back in her lap. This is very important to her because most women have a tendency to be overly responsible. The more complex and stressful their lives become, the more overwhelmed and exhausted they become.

A woman begins to feel responsible for doing everything for everyone. Her way of getting relief is to share these feelings with someone she loves. If she can share, something happens inside her and she doesn't feel so responsible. It is as if she sees all possible problems and, unless she tells someone, it is up to her to solve them.

She can begin to relax when she feels that she is being heard; then she knows that if he can do anything to be of assistance, he will do what he can. Most important, she has been able to talk about it. For her, that is the most important part of a man's support.

DECEMBER 30

Learning to Receive

"*N*eeding" is openly reaching out and asking for support from a man in a trusting manner that assumes he will do his best. This approach empowers him. "Neediness" is desperately seeking support even though you're not sure you will get it. It pushes men away and makes them feel rejected and unappreciated.

For women, not only is needing others confusing, but being disappointed or abandoned is especially painful, even in the smallest ways. It is not easy for a woman to depend on others and then be ignored, forgotten, or dismissed. Needing others puts her in a vulnerable position.

Being ignored or disappointed hurts more because it affirms the incorrect belief that she is unworthy.

When a woman realizes that she deserves to be loved, she is opening the door for a man to give to her. When it takes her ten years of overgiving in a marriage to realize that she deserves more, she feels like closing the door and not giving him the chance. She may feel something like this: "I have given to you and you have ignored me. You had your chance. I deserve better. I can't trust you. I am too tired, I have nothing left to give. I will not let you hurt me again."

Quite often, when one partner makes a positive change, the other will also change. When your partner makes a positive change, make sure that you are open to seeing it and trusting it. Change is always fragile; it needs to be encouraged, not tested. Don't let your baggage or mistrust push your partner away. By staying open to the possibility of positive change, you become like a magnet attracting exactly what you want and need.

When the student is ready, the teacher appears. This predictable coincidence is one of those magical things in life. When the question is asked, the answer is heard. When we are truly open to receive, then what we need will become available. When the Venusians are ready to receive, the Martians are ready to give.

December 31

Real and Lasting Love

*F*inding true and lasting love doesn't mean we will be able to feel it all the time. Everything in the world moves in cycles. Night follows day, the tide moves out and then in, what goes up eventually comes down. Likewise, when the heart opens, it also closes. The commitment of marriage helps us each time to open our hearts once again. Each time we act and react in a manner that will keep this commitment of the soul, we once again open our hearts and align ourselves with our highest purpose.

Vermilion Books are available from all good bookshops
or call the TBS Direct mail order hotline on:
01206 255 800

Postage and Packing is free